Angel Investing by the Numbers

Other Books by Hambleton Lord
and Christopher Mirabile

Fundamentals of Angel Investing
A Guide to the Principles, Skills and Concepts Every Investor Needs to Succeed

Leaders Wanted: Making Startup Deals Happen
Advanced Techniques in Deal Leadership and Due Diligence for Early Stage Investors

Guide, Advise, Inspire
How Startup Boards Drive Growth and Exits

Angel Investing by the Numbers

Valuation, Capitalization,
Portfolio Construction and Startup Economics

Hambleton Lord
Christopher Mirabile

Seraf
Compass
Publications

www.seraf-investor.com

Copyright © 2017 by Seraf LLC

All rights reserved. No part of this publication may be reproduced, distributed, or transmitted in any form or by any means, including photocopying, recording, or other electronic or mechanical methods, without the prior written permission of the publisher, except in the case of brief quotations embodied in critical reviews and certain other noncommercial uses permitted by copyright law. For permission requests, contact the publisher, addressed "Attention: Permissions Coordinator," at the address below.

support@seraf-investor.com

www.seraf-investor.com

Table of Contents

1. Understanding Early Stage Capitalization Tables   5
2. Methods for Valuing Startups   19
3. Startup Pathways to Success   61
4. Building a Startup Portfolio That Will Get You There   73
5. The Mix of a Winning Startup Portfolio   85
6. Understanding Stock Options and Restricted Stock   93

Appendix

I. Capitalization Table with Waterfall Analysis   113
II. Portfolio Modeling Tool   119
III. IRS Section 83(b) Election Form   123

The Results Oriented Approach to Early Stage Investing

In the sport of Major League Baseball, the greatest hitters are those who get a hit just one out of every three times at bat and a home run 5 or 6 times out of 100 at bats. In the world of startup company investing, the best-known investors are those who invest in the tiny percentage of companies that make it big. Think Facebook, Google or Amazon. If you invest in one of those enormously successful companies you will find your name in the equivalent of the Baseball Hall of Fame… it's called the Forbes Midas List.

To continue the analogy, the most famous investors don't worry about getting on base. In fact, their batting average might be quite low. They are so successful because they swing for the fences every time they get up to bat, and they are able to connect for the rare grand slam.

It is tempting to think that is the only way to succeed. And maybe if you are trying to build a reputation as the best home run hitter in baseball it is. But if you are trying to field a winning team over the course of a long season, it is not the only way.

The principles popularized by Michael Lewis' book MoneyBall illustrate a different and less dramatic way. An approach of chipping away at the problem, making every position and every at bat count for as much as it can. Efficiency and economy in playing style rather than flamboyance.

So which is the right method for an angel looking for long term returns? Should a typical angel investor apply the "swing for the fences" approach to their personal investing? After all, if you make just one hugely successful investment in your portfolio, you will make up for dozens of failed investments. But, the likelihood of investing in the biggest winners is quite low - too low to bank on. Further, some of the biggest winners come in the consumer space where there is a global market, but a lot of consumer fickleness. Those deals have an element of risk that is almost impossible to be compensated for taking on.

Therefore, our personal strategy for angel investing isn't 100% focused on the hunt for the biggest winners. We always love when we find such investments, but we are realists and understand that, on a day-to-day, year-to-year basis we need to take a different approach to building our angel investment portfolios. Our strategy is more akin to the MoneyBall "efficiency and economy" approach to investing. We don't try to wait for the perfect pitch and rely on grand slams, we try to accumulate lots of doubles, triples and the occasional home runs. If the bases happen to be loaded when we get one, great, but we don't bet the portfolio on it.

So how does this actually work in real life? From reading some of our other books, you know we love to invest in great teams, going after big markets with great new solutions to the customer's problem. But it goes beyond those basics. Here, we will discuss what investors should know about the financial mechanics of angel investing. Just like the baseball team manager using a MoneyBall approach needs to really understand the statistics of the game, the successful investor employing our approach needs to understand the financial mechanics of investing.

In the following chapters we will cover important topics such as:

- How do you read and understand a Capitalization Table?
- How do you place a value on an early stage company with a limited track record?
- What are some of the financial paths that lead to a successful exit for angel investors?
- How do you construct your portfolio to improve the likelihood of successful returns?
- What does the underlying financial math look like in a top tier angel portfolio?
- What approaches do you use to exercise options and buy restricted stock that minimize taxes and optimize your financial outcome?

Having a solid understanding of valuations, exit paths and portfolio construction might not sound like as much fun as baseball for many of our readers. But trust us, after investing in startups for a combined 25+ years and 100+ companies, Christopher and I have learned the hard way and fully embrace the importance of mastering these important topics. Just because finance wasn't an interest in your career doesn't mean you can ignore the financial mechanics of angel investing.... unless, of course, you get lucky and invest in the next Amazon!

Chapter 1

Who Owns What - Understanding Early Stage Capitalization Tables

Several years ago, I was speaking to a colleague of mine. He was trying to decide between two great job offers, and was having a difficult time making a final decision. When I asked him questions about work environment, the quality of his co-workers and boss, and the future potential for the companies, he responded that both companies fit what he was looking for.

Next, I started asking about his compensation package. For salary and bonus, the two companies were equivalent. However, when it came to stock, there seemed to be a big difference. One company offered him 25,000 shares that vested over a 3 year period. The other company offered 300,000 shares that vested over 4 years. Because one offer was almost twelve times greater than the other offer, my friend felt he should take the job from the company that was giving him more shares. His decision was a pretty typical response from someone without much financial experience.

So I asked him a simple question. "Do you know how many shares each company has issued?" His face went blank and he shook his head 'no'. He had no clue what I was talking about. I paused for a minute and then asked my question in a different way. "Do you know how big a slice of the company pie you are getting from Company A vs. Company B?"

Now I could see the wheels turning in his head. "Ahh, I get it", he replied. "I don't know the answer to that question, but I will ask each company and get back to you with the answer." The next day he texted me and told me that the 25,000 share offer was equivalent to a bit more than 1% of the company's total outstanding shares. The 300,000 share offer was about a half percent of that company's shares. So even though one offer looked very generous compared to the other, in reality, the smaller share offer represented more than twice the ownership position of the bigger share offer.

> **We spend time modeling future cap tables for our investments, helping us understand what happens over time as companies raise additional rounds of financing.**

I tell this story as one simple example of the importance of actually understanding a company's Capitalization Table ("cap table") before transacting in their shares. Shareholders who don't have a good grasp of this important investment concept are at a significant handicap when it comes to investing. If you don't know what you own, how can you understand either its value today or its potential value in the future?

Ham and I spend a lot of time thinking about cap tables, making sure we understand what our ownership position will be after we invest in a company. Furthermore, we spend time modeling future cap tables for our investments, helping us understand what happens over time as companies raise additional rounds of financing. Let's ask Ham for a little more about the basics of this so you can wrap your head around what we consider to be one of the most important concepts of early stage investing.

Q

Ham, to start out, what is a Cap Table? Can you give us a simple definition?

Whenever I hear the term "cap table", I can't help but envision an accountant wearing a green eyeshade hunched over a giant ledger. In this ledger is a listing of all the shareholders and security holders in the company tallied up to make sure that the company's share count equals the total number of shares held by the sum of all the investors and other security holders such as managers, founders, paid advisors and employees. In summary, that's what a cap table represents - it is a table illustrating the capitalization of the company.

To be a bit more specific, the cap table tracks the equity ownership of all the company's shareholders and security holders and the value assigned to this equity. In case it is not clear, cap tables need to be comprehensive. They should include all elements of company stakeholders such as convertible debt, stock options and warrants in addition to common and preferred stock.

Typically built and stored in a spreadsheet, the cap table is one of the most critical documents maintained by the company. I can't stress enough the importance of accuracy with this document. I highly recommend that an investor spend some time reviewing the company's cap table and making sure their ownership position is fairly represented. If it isn't, you will need to reach out to the company and make sure any appropriate corrections are made in a timely fashion.

Since we are talking about numbers, I think it helps to see what a basic cap table looks like. Here is a very simple example. The table below highlights the most basic information in a cap table. For example, if you are Investor One, you own 500,000 shares of Series A Preferred stock. The company has the right to issue up to 4,000,000 shares including the option pool, so on a fully diluted basis (i.e. pretending all the options were granted), your holdings are equivalent to 12.5% of all the shares of the company.

To help you get started modeling a company's cap table, we've provided two examples you can copy and experiment with (see the Appendix for more details). These spreadsheets will help you model single round and multi-round

Name	Common Stock	Stock Options	Series A Preferred	Total Shares	Percent Outstanding	Percent Fully Diluted
Founder One	1,500,000		250,000	1,750,000	47.0%	43.7%
Founder Two	1,100,000			1,100,000	29.6%	27.5%
Employee One		80,000		80,000	2.2%	2.0%
Employee Two		40,000		40,000	1.1%	1.0%
Investor One			500,000	500,000	13.4%	12.5%
Investor Two			250,000	250,000	6.7%	6.3%
Remaining Option Pool		280,000		280,000		7.0%
Total	2,600,000	400,000	1,000,000	4,000,000	100%	100%
Percent Ownership	65%	10%	25%	100%		

[handwritten at top: Is the total # of shares set at the begining? Can it change?]

financings and include features such as options, liquidation preferences, participating preferred and the resulting waterfall analysis.

Q

What are the key terms used in cap table analysis that every investor must understand?

If you want to be an effective investor, it's important for you to be able to speak fluently the language found in a cap table. To get you up the curve faster, we'll break the key terms used in cap tables into three categories: ==Valuations, Security Types and Share Counts==.

Valuations

- ==**Pre-Money Valuation**== - This is the valuation placed on the company prior to an investment made in the company. This valuation is typically set through a negotiation between the investors and company management. We discuss how this valuation is set in great detail in Chapter 2.

- **Post-Money Valuation** - This is the effective valuation of the company after an investment is made in the comoany. For example, if the pre-money valuation is $3M and the investors make a $1M investment, the post-money valuation is $4M (the $3M *[pre-val]* value plus the $1M in liquid cash—*[investmt]* now on the balance sheet).

- **Price per Share** - This is a calculation based on taking the post-money valuation and dividing it by the number of fully diluted shares. If we have a $8M post-money valuation and we have 4 million shares, the price per share is $2.

[margin note: post / fully diluted share]

Security Types

- **Common Stock** - The most basic form of equity ownership in a company is called common stock. Each share of common stock represents partial ownership of the company and gives the shareholder certain rights to company profits and voting on corporate matters, all as spelled out in the charter and the law of the state of incorporation.

- **Preferred Stock** - A class or series of stock with <u>special rights and privileges outlined in the</u> company's charter. <u>By default, preferred stock is typically paid before common (but after debt)</u> in a liquidation or sale situation.

- **Convertible Preferred Stock** - This is <u>preferred stock which has the option to convert to common stock (and be paid at the same time and rate as common)</u> under a <u>specified set of circumstances</u>, including at the holder's discretion.

- **Participating Preferred** - <u>This is a type of preferred stock which has the right to be paid some multiple of the original purchase price (e.g. 1X) and then also convert to common stock and "participate" in the distribution to common</u> as if it had simply converted in the first place.

- **Non-participating Preferred** - This is a type of preferred stock which has the right to be paid some multiple of the original purchase price (e.g. 1X) OR convert to common stock and "participate" in the distribution to common. The investor will choose the liquidity method that delivers the greatest financial return. This can also be referred to as just "preferred stock" but calling it "non-participating preferred" avoids all doubt about what kind it is.

- **Stock Options** - A stock option is a contractual right to purchase a specified number of shares for a specified price at a specified future date or dates. Stock options are typically issued under the terms of a stock option plan out of a pre-approved pool of shares set aside for options and restricted stock grants. i.e. *employees*

- **Warrants** - Warrants are nearly the same as options in that they are a <u>contractual right to purchase a specified number of shares for a specified price at a specified future date or dates</u>. Unlike stock options, warrants are typically one-offs and not issued under the terms of the stock option plan, though they may or may not use shares set aside in the option pool. Options are commonly used as compensation for employees and <u>warrants tend to be used</u>

10

more frequently in business transaction contexts.

- **Restricted Stock** - Restricted stock is increasingly used instead of options because of its greater potential tax efficiency. With options, you do not actually own the stock until vesting occurs and you exercise the stock option. Restricted shares are granted up front, but that up-front ownership is subject to restrictions which fall away over time. In other words, options have ownership *rights* which vest over time, restricted shares have ownership *restrictions* which lapse over time. The key difference is tax efficiency - restricted shares allow the recipient to make an election under Section 83(b) and pay a small amount of taxes up front in order to access the lower capital gains rate on any future profits.

Share Counts

- **Authorized Shares** - All shares in a company must be properly authorized before they are issued (as in the context of a financing). Authorized shares refer to that number of shares which has been duly authorized by the company's board for present or future issuance.

- **Outstanding Shares** - This is the total number of shares which have actually been issued. It does not include options which have not been granted, nor does it include granted options which have not been exercised, since the shares are only issued upon exercise.

- **Fully Diluted Shares** - This is a calculated number which models all granted options, restricted stock, warrants and often the remainder of the option pool itself into one single number of shares that represents the theoretical count if all outstanding contingencies were granted and exercised.

Q

How do these cap tables evolve over time? What events result in a change to an early stage company's cap table?

When a company is first incorporated, the cap table is pretty simple. Let's say you have two company founders. At that time, the cap table will have some common shares issued to the founders, and that's it. Simple!

> As the company adds employees, directors and advisors, it will typically create and grant options, restricted stock awards or warrants from an "option pool" as a way to attract, incentivize and retain those people.

Over time the cap table will necessarily become more complex. I like to think of changes to the cap table occurring based on two different groups: (1) New Employees, Directors and Advisors and (2) New Investors (and if they are given securities such as warrants, Creditors).

Employees, Directors and Advisors

As the company adds employees, directors and advisors, it will typically create and grant options, restricted stock awards or warrants from an "option pool" as a way to attract, incentivize and retain those people. Option pools vary in size, but are typically designed to represent somewhere between 5% and 25% of the total outstanding shares of the company.

Here are some examples of the employee, director and advisor events that will result in a change to or notation on the cap table:

- Establishing an option pool (more authorized shares if insufficient shares authorized, new line item on the cap table)

- Increasing the size of the option pool (more authorized shares, increase in the pool line item)

- Issuing an option grant, restricted share award or warrant to an individual, e.g. employee, director, advisor (new line item for the options, reduction in size of remaining pool)

How are fully outstanding shares determined? (handwritten)

- Exercising of options or warrants by an individual (reduction of their option listing, increase in common stockholder list and common shares outstanding)

- Terminating unvested options, unvested restricted share awards or expired warrants when an individual's service to the company ends before options are vested (removal of an option line item, and typically a return of those shares to the pool)

- Any transfer of shares between an individual and another entity e.g. an investor or the company (a boost in shares issued and a new line item for that investor)

> When capital is raised, it can take the form of either equity (partial ownership of the company) or convertible debt or straight debt with warrants (lender). In either case, this information should be recorded on the cap table.

Investors and Creditors

Most early stage companies raise capital from a variety of sources over time including friends, family, angels and VCs. When capital is raised, it can take the form of either equity (partial ownership of the company) or convertible debt or straight debt with warrants (lender). *(handwritten: equity, convertible debt)* In either case, this information should be recorded on the cap table. Here is a list of the events that will result in a change to the cap table due to raising either equity or debt:

- Selling new shares of an existing security, e.g. common shares (new line item for that shareholder, reduction in pool of authorized but unissued shares)

- Selling new shares of a new security, e.g. a new series of preferred shares (creation of a new class, often reflected in a new column on the cap table for clarity, plus new line items for the new investors)

- Issuing convertible debt through some form of note. Even though issuing debt typically does not result in an immediate issuance of shares, it's important to record this information because it will lead to the issuance of shares or may have payment priority so it can affect an investor's ultimate payout upon a company exit (new line item to reflect this debt and signal its potential impact for full dilution calculations)

- Issuing warrants as part of either a debt or equity round of financing (new line item, possible reduction of the option pool if the warrants use the pool)

Debt is paid first

> **Remember that in almost all liquidation situations, debt holders are paid first before any proceeds can be paid out to equity holders.**

The above lists are not a full set of all the events that can impact a cap table, but they cover the most common events in early stage companies and give you a sense of the landscape. We can't emphasize enough the importance of a company recording any events that might impact a cap table. If a company and its investors don't have a good handle on company ownership, they may run into serious legal issues down the road, including the potential for fraud claims.

So what are Convertible Notes? How do they affect the cap table?

Convertible notes are debt, but a special kind of debt that is not meant to be paid back in cash. Instead, it is meant to convert into shares of the company at some future date. So it blends concepts of both debt and equity. Regardless of whether it has converted or not, it is important for the cap table. Remember that in almost all liquidation situations, debt holders are paid first before any proceeds can be paid out to equity holders. Therefore, you need to know how much debt is outstanding, whether any of it is convertible, and what the terms of conversion are, before you can fully understand how big a slice of the pie you will ultimately end up with. All debt should be recorded in a section of the cap table.

It is helpful to include the following information in the cap table document so you will understand how much equity might be issued to note holders at some point in the future:

* Date the debt was incurred
* Amount of indebtedness
* Interest rate
* Interest rate calculation mechanism (annual, semi-annual, cumulative, non-cumulative)
* Maturity date (due date)
* Terms and conditions driving conversion.

Then usually immediately after those terms there will be some discussion of any financial terms relating to conversion, such as a negotiated cap on the conversion price or discount against the conversion price if the deal features a cap or discount.

It is not uncommon for an early stage company to raise more than $1M using convertible notes. That amount can represent a significant position on the cap table once it has been converted, so make sure you keep track of it.

> **A common feature found in preferred stock is the liquidation preference. This feature of preferred stock gives the preferred shareholders the right to get paid a specified amount before common stockholders.**

Q

Ok, so those are the basics, but what are some additional early stage deal terms that can affect the cap table?

The two biggies are the liquidation preference and the anti-dilution provisions.

A common feature found in preferred stock is the liquidation preference. This feature of preferred stock gives the preferred shareholders the right in a liquidation to be paid a specified amount before common stockholders are paid anything. The liquidation preference is typically expressed as a multiple (e.g. 1X, 2X, etc.) of the amount of the investor's original investment. For example a 1X preference gives the investor the right to get one times their money back before any distributions to other shareholders with lower priority.

To shed some light on this term, let's give a simple example:

- Suppose you own the less-common and more investor-friendly form of preferred stock, participating preferred, with a 1X liquidation preference.

- You invested $1M at a $4M pre-money, so you own 20% of the company.

- If the company is acquired for $10M you would expect to be entitled to 20% of that $10M, or $2M, but it is not that simple because of the terms of the deal; instead, your payout is as follows...

- First, you get paid your liquidation preference. In this case, that is equal to $1M (i.e.

one times the amount of your original investment.)

- Next, you get paid 20% of the remaining value of the company. In this case that will be 20% of $9M or a total of $1.8M

- Your total payout is $2.8M. That equals 28% of the acquisition price for the company. So that 1X liquidation preference had a pretty large effect on your ultimate returns in this example.

The other biggie is the anti-dilution provision. This is a provision which acts like a "magic" adjustable price for shares. Shares which come with anti-dilution protection have the right to be repriced downward in the event that later shares in the company are offered in the future at a lower price. Exactly how they are repriced can be complicated (most deals specify that a broad-based weighted-average calculation be used and that additional shares be granted as the mechanism for "repricing"), but for our purposes, the details of precise calculation don't matter. What matters is that if the transaction for which you are analyzing the cap table is not an upwardly priced round and might trigger anti-dilution provisions, a whole bunch of shares may flood into the cap table analysis as compensation to those folks on the lines where the relevant shares are located.

> Over time, complexity is added to the cap table as you raise capital, incur debt and hire employees. Understanding the effects of liquidation preferences, dividends, interest, warrants, etc. can be quite complex. That's where a waterfall analysis comes into play.

Also, an important reminder: one frequently-overlooked term is the dividend. Sometimes there is a dividend quietly ticking away and accruing (either on a cumulative or non-cumulative basis) to the benefit of one or more classes of preferred stock. Many exits end up taking far longer than anyone originally anticipated. In these cases, having a dividend accumulating in the background can make an enormous difference in the ultimate ownership (and returns) of the different classes of stock. For example, using the rule of 72, an 8% dividend alone will give you a 2X return all by itself if left to run for 9 years. So make sure the cap table indicates or you research which securities are paying dividends and what the start date is on payment of those dividends.

Q

This is getting complicated. I hear the term "waterfall analysis" used a lot by some experienced angel investors in my community. Is that what we are talking about here? What is the purpose of a waterfall analysis for an early stage investor?

At the beginning of this chapter, I showed a very simple cap table. It's extremely rare for an early stage company to get all the way to an exit with such a simple cap table. Over time, complexity is added to the cap table as you raise capital, incur debt and hire employees. Understanding the effects of liquidation preferences, dividends, interest, warrants, etc. can be quite complex. That's where a waterfall analysis comes into play.

A waterfall analysis is the technical term used to describe the process of calculating exact amounts each shareholder and debt holder will be paid upon any liquidation event of the company (e.g. an acquisition, an IPO, etc.). Basically it is just a sequential series of calculations where you apply the various deal terms to the cap table in the order required to flow the whole thing through to the end.

If you are interested in digging deeper to understand how the waterfall analysis works, take a look at our example cap table (see the appendix). We have a separate tab in this spreadsheet called "Waterfall Analysis". This shows you an approach for modeling a variety of exit scenarios.

There are so many variables that drive the eventual outcome of your investment in an early stage company. If you are lucky and invest in the next Facebook, you won't worry about dividends, warrants and liquidation preferences. They don't matter all that much in such a huge exit. But for the more typical exit, where a company is acquired for less than $100M, these terms do matter. So make sure you grasp the basic concepts and you will become a better investor.

Chapter 2

Approximations, Assumptions and Aspirations: Methods For Valuing Startups

Over the years, Christopher and I have interacted with hundreds of startups. Whether as an advisor, mentor, investor or just as an observer, the issue of valuation has been a major part of our conversation with each of these companies. And, given how widely reasonable people can differ on this subjective topic, I have to admit, it can be one of the most difficult, contentious conversations you will have as an investor.

Think about it. You are giving the entrepreneur advice on how to value her startup. The lower the price, the better the deal is for you, the investor. That doesn't sound like an unbiased conversation to me. And it sure doesn't sound unbiased to the entrepreneur.

So let's ask Christopher how he goes about the process of determining a reasonable valuation for an early stage company and then manages the discussion with the entrepreneur so that both sides end up in a good place.

Q

Christopher, what is so hard about valuing a startup company?

How do you value an early stage technology company that has a partially completed product, no revenue and three employees? How about just two engineers, a Powerpoint slide deck and an office mascot? If the founders in these example companies tried to sell their businesses out-right, they would be lucky to get anything for them.

> **The valuation does not have to be precise or perfect, but it has to be close enough to get the gears of commerce turning.**

A great idea with no market validation may have plenty of future potential but is worth almost nothing at inception. Backing it with a team capable of executing helps a bit, but you still can't value the business on financial metrics. No revenue means no revenue multiple. It also means no EBITDA, and therefore no EBITDA multiple. A price-sales multiple gets you to zero, as well. So obviously, we have to come up with another approach to placing a fair value on the company that will ultimately result in a successful financial outcome for both the entrepreneurs and the investors.

The valuation does not have to be precise or perfect, but it has to be close enough to get the gears of commerce turning. To the extent there is some imprecision, you might be surprised to learn the benefit of that imprecision is virtually always in the entrepreneur's favor. How could that be, you might ask, given the relative power imbalance with investors having the money startups need? It boils down to the realities of startup life and cap table math. The first financing round valuation generally needs to be above what the company is really worth to make the "founder economics" work.

Q

What do you mean by "above what the company is really worth"?

Building a startup is a really hard, risky and initially low-paying job. Most people who choose to do it are motivated, at least in part, by the long-term view that their startup stock will be worth a great deal down the road. That gives them the motivation to start, and the will to continue on, despite the risk, the low pay, the opportunity cost of market salary jobs passed by, and the frustrations and difficulties of getting the product built and into the hands of customers.

Given that long term stock appreciation is the motivating factor, it's vitally important to make sure the founding team retains a good chunk of ownership in the company. And there is the rub. Two engineers, a Powerpoint business plan, and a dog aren't really worth anything in a present value sense. Nobody would pay much to buy that package as an out-right buyer. But that same team needs serious money to get off the ground and become a company. And the founders need to be motivated. ==So there is little choice but to assign a somewhat artificially high valuation at the first round.==

Let's look at the math. Suppose you have three founders owning 33% each of a company which needs $1.5M to get off the ground. You assign a pre-money valuation that is an accurate reflection of the true value of the "assets" of the company (team, Powerpoint, dog). To be overly-generous we'll say $100,000. So the investors put up the $1.5M, at a pre-money of $100,000. The investors would end up owning 93.75% of the company on a post-money basis and the founders would each own 2.1%. And, that's before creating an option pool or taking on subsequent dilution from raising additional rounds of financing. That just is not enough incentive for founders to quit their current jobs, risk their mortgages or other financial commitments, and take on the uncertainty and hassle of founding and growing a startup.

> **The key point to understand is that, with equity investing, having a valuation ascribed each time needed resources come in and shares go out is the fulcrum on which the entire process balances.**

So a different and less accurate, but more pragmatic valuation has to be assigned. To help you figure out how to assign such a valuation we are going to take a look at the different methods out there, explain some of their shortcomings, and propose an alternate method we developed over years of trial and error and we think works more reliably.

Q

Before we delve into valuation approaches, can you provide us with a brief explanation as to why setting a fair valuation on a company is treated with such great importance by both the investor and the entrepreneur?

Equity investing as a mechanism is really genius if you stop to think about it. It is sort of the keystone of modern capitalism. Can you think of a more perfect mechanism to align interests, allocate risks and share upside than to divvy up the ownership of a company into infinitely divisible shares and give those shares to the different stakeholders in proportion to the contribution they've made? With the simplest equity deal, nobody wins unless everybody wins, and risk of failure is borne by all in proportion to their ownership.

The key point to understand is that, with equity investing, having a valuation ascribed each time needed resources come in and shares go out is the fulcrum on which the entire process balances. Companies need resources (money) to grow. They get those resources in exchange for a percentage of ownership (i.e. a share of the upside and the downside). The valuation set on the company as the resources are coming in determines what percentage of the company is given for those resources. The challenge is that the valuation is subjective. And the challenge is compounded by the fact that everyone involved needs to agree - both all past contributors of value, and the present potential contributors (for example, every participant in a financing round). Getting all that done in a somewhat efficient manner can be fiendishly complex.

Fortunately there are some norms and practices that make it easier to navigate, and there are also some harsh realities which constrain the valuation ranges quite a bit. Investors who do these kinds of deals all the time generally have a pretty good handle on these issues. Entrepreneurs may only do it a handful of times in their career and may need some help. This is one of the main reasons I view valuation discussions as more of an education process than a negotiation. A big part of what I am doing is explaining the realities of the situation and helping the entrepreneur appreciate the constraints - those on them and those on me.

Q

What kinds of realities are you talking about in these valuation discussions?

It is pretty simple, really. There are two main constraints:

- What the current investor "market" will bear

- What this transaction is likely to do to the company's position in the future.

Current market conditions boil down to the tension between what the founders and existing stockholders will give up to get more resources, and what the investors are willing to contribute for a certain amount of stock. Is this a hot, in-demand deal with lots of attractive features, or does this company have some drawbacks? We will talk a great deal more about this later in the chapter.

> Current market conditions boil down to the tension between what the founders and existing stockholders will give up to get more resources, and what the investors are willing to contribute for a certain amount of stock.

Future market conditions require speculation about where the company will be when this money runs out and what the next valuation give-and-take might look like at that time. This should be a vitally important question to investors and it is one to which Ham and I feel people don't pay enough attention.

To illustrate why this is so important, let's give an example I have used many times before. If the company needs $1M now, the founders (and any existing investors) might be willing to give up a quarter of the company to get that $1M. In other words, they might agree to a $3M pre-money valuation to get $1M in the door (resulting in a $4M post-money and 25% ownership for the new investors.) If the investors are willing to put up that $1M in exchange for 25%, then you have a deal that works under current market conditions.

But one of the things that influences (or should influence) the investor's decision about whether to accept 25% (or put the money up at all) is speculation about future market conditions. Investors understand that they will be heading into uncharted waters. They know that $1M is almost certainly not the only money this company is going to need. Growth consumes cash. The company will have to go back out into the market for more money. And at that time, a new valuation process will begin. Experienced investors know that by coming in on an early round, you are not only assuming the risk of company failure, you are assuming the risk that future rounds might be offered on unattractive terms, even if the business has not completely failed.

So the smart investor asks herself "What will that process look like? Might future investors be unwilling to give as good a deal as we are?" At the present moment there is clarity. Everyone agrees that the morning after they do the $1M/$3M deal, the company will indisputably be worth $4M because they just valued it at $3M at arms' length and it has $1M of cash on the balance sheet.

But what about the future? The company plans to take that $1M off the balance sheet and spend it on people, product and progress. The critical question is this:

Will the company still be worth at least $4M once it doesn't have $1M in cash on the balance sheet?

That is the key question because, if the company is not worth $4M next time it goes out for money, it may not be able to raise money again on good terms. If future investors are not impressed with where the company is at, they might offer poor terms. Not only will the current investors experience the normal expected arithmetic dilution from the future round, they will also experience economic dilution. Economic dilution is caused by a new round with a pre-money that is below the post-money on the previous round. Not only is their percentage stake smaller, it is also *worth* less than it was before. (For more on this distinction between arithmetic and economic dilution, see later in the chapter.)

Q

So what does that mean in terms of arriving at a valuation?

If you follow the logic of this all the way through, you arrive at a key insight: ***it is really the post-money valuation that matters***. Even though all the discussion will be about the $3M pre-money, the experienced investors are all focused on the $4M post-money. They are making a bet that this team can combine what it has with the $1M investment and build a $4M+ company before that $1M is gone. So what appears to be a discussion about how much of the company the investors get for their $1M is really a speculation about whether the company can get where it needs to be before it is forced to be re-valued by the market.

If the assessment is that the company can make some value-inflecting progress like finishing the product, racking up a convincing number of initial sales, showing some good unit economics on each transaction, and building its team, then maybe investors will accept a $3M pre-money and a $4M post-money. But if the work to be done is too daunting to accomplish with that $1M, investors have two choices.

Option one is to pay a lower valuation. This accomplishes two things:

- It gives the investors a greater percentage ownership of the company to reward them for taking the risk, and insulates them against likely future dilution. So for example, they might give a $2M valuation which would mean they own 33% rather than 25%.

- It lowers the post-money valuation to $3M instead of $4M, making it far more likely that the company can get a future round done at a valuation that is flat or positive relative to the new post-money of $3M.

Option two is a little bit counterintuitive. If you are worried about the post-money, the alternative option is to give the company more money. This is counterintuitive and risky because it drives the post-money up even farther. But, it gives the company more resources to achieve what it must achieve before going out to raise again. For example, instead of giving $1M on $3M pre-money, assume the investors give $1.5M on a $3M pre-money. Instead of owning 25% at a post-money valuation of $4M, they now own 33% of a $4.5M post-money ($1.5M of $4.5M). Investors get higher percentage ownership by providing the company with more runway to hit key milestones.

If there is sufficient investor demand to come up with the extra money, this second alternative can be a great path forward. It is like the difference between playing offense and defense. Lowering the valuation is a defensive move - biding your time and letting things play out carefully without sticking your neck out too far on post-money. Increasing the size of the round is an offensive move. You are compounding the post-money problem if the bet is wrong, but you are bringing in more resources for the team to succeed and you are owning a bigger slice of the company.

As you can see from this example, figuring out the round size and getting valuation as close to "correct" as you can matters a lot to both sets of stakeholders. If you put it too high, the company may not be able to raise again, or may be forced to raise on very weak terms that hurt everyone. But if you put it too low, the founders (and possibly other early investors) who took all the risk of getting this started might give too much away and lack motivation to continue when the going gets rough.

Closing reminder: valuation is not the only term in a deal. There are lots of other tools used to allocate various risks, but to keep the example clear, we are focusing on the valuation question.

Q

OK, so finding the right valuation is really hard, somewhat arbitrary and yet really important. How do investors do it? What are some of the most common approaches you've seen applied to valuing early stage companies?

It is anyone's guess how valuations have historically been derived in the most informal parts of the angel investing world, where one-off founders and one-off investors just try to get a business launched. I suspect people approximate and try to see what feels fair and reasonable and let the chips fall where they may (probably learning hard lessons in the process). But in the more organized angel investing world, where investors do a lot of deals that are focused on high-growth, high-potential startups, there are four slightly more formal methods that have been predominate. Each method is quite straightforward and easy to explain to both investors and entrepreneurs. But, each method has drawbacks. I will explain those in a moment, in addition to suggesting a better approach. But let me summarize these four methods first.

Four Traditional Methods For Valuing Start-Ups

The first three out of the four start with the notion of adding and subtracting value based on a variety of factors. Let's start with what is commonly referred to as the **Berkus Method**, named after my friend and colleague and well-known angel investor Dave Berkus. In the Berkus Method, you basically look at five aspects of the company and assign some value to each one:

Berkus Method	
If it Exists:	**Add to Company Value:**
Sound Idea	$500,000
Product Prototype	$500,000
Quality Team	$500,000
Quality Board	$500,000
Initial Sales	$500,000

As you can see, this method accounts for some of the main risk factors and attempts to give an admittedly arbitrary value in exchange for ticking the boxes on each one. A user of this model can refine it by changing the amount added across the board to reflect higher or lower prevailing average market valuations (i.e. have the factors add up to something different than $2.5M), but overall it is a relatively easy, rugged and somewhat over-simplified model.

In recognition of the limitations of the Berkus Method, my friend and colleague and well-known angel investor Bill Payne set out to improve on it with what he called the "==Scorecard Method==." Bill essentially asked "What if we look at more factors, give each one a relative weighting to reflect its importance, and a rating to score how well the company does on that factor?" So, for example a company might get a minor ding in valuation for scoring poorly on an unimportant factor, and a bigger ding for scoring poorly on an important one.

The Payne Scorecard Method then goes to pick an arbitrary starting point or "pre-money multiplier" of, for example, $2.25M, then takes the weighted average of the factors and multiplies it against the pre-money multiplier. So in the example above, the weighted average rating works out to 1.0875, which you then multiply by the pre-money multiplier to come up with a pre-money of $2,446,875 (or 1.0875 x $2.25M).

As you can see from the table, this method brings a few more factors into play, and allows you to fine tune it with both weighting and scores, but it still leaves a lot of key issues out and relies on a tremendous amount of subjectivity. Plus, you still have to pick an arbitrary pre-money multiplier in the first place!

Scorecard Method

Factor	Weight	Rating	Comment
Management	30	125	Full team
Size of Opportunity	25	115	Could be huge
Product/Service	10	110	Disruptive platform
Sales Channels	10	70	All foreign
Stage of Business	10	125	Prototype works
Other	15	80	Revenue non US

The third method is yet another incremental improvement on the Berkus and Payne approaches - it takes concepts from both and combines them. This method is called the **Risk Factor Summation Method** and simply takes a similar pre-money starting point, adds a longer list of factors and allows you to score each factor on a scale of +$500K to -$500K. So using the same example:

Once you net out the rating column at +$250K, you add that to the pre-money starting point of $2.25M and come up with a pre-money valuation of $2.5M.

Again, the Risk Factor Summation Method is an improvement in both sophistication and granularity, but still feels a bit arbitrary given that you have to pick a starting point and decide how much to add to each factor.

Risk Factor Summation Method

Risk Factor	Rating (-$500k to +$500k)	Comment
Management	+$500k	Done it before
Stage	+$250k	Prototype works
Funding Risk	-$250k	Market tough
Regulatory	0	Unregulated market
Manufacturing	+$250k	Nothing new
Sales & Marketing	-$500k	Intl markets
Competition	+$250k	Few in target market
Technology	+$250k	Off shelf parts
Litigation	0	None anticipated
International	-$500k	All revs international
Reputation	-$250k	International issues
Exit	+$250k	Likely early
	= +$250K	

The fourth method is one angels have borrowed from the VC industry and so it is typically referred to as the **Venture Capital Method**. As Bill Payne explains it, the Venture Capital Method is all about projecting a future state and then working backwards from there to derive your required valuation.

Here's an example: let's say a company needs $1M, and we assume it will exit by M&A in year 5. Let's further assume it will have revenue of $20M that fifth year (optimistic, but certainly possible.) And we will assume it will have net profit of 10% or $2M which will yield it a somewhat economically standard P/E ratio of 15X.

That means that the company would be worth $30M on exit (i.e. 15 P/E ratio x $2M in earnings). If investors require a cash-on-cash return of 10 times their money, then the value of their stake in the company must be $10M at exit ($1M investment x 10). If they need $10M out of a $30M exit, that is one third, so they need to own 33% of the company. Therefore, if they are putting in $1M, and need to own a third, then the pre-money must be set at $2M. Here it is in table format:

Venture Capital Method

Investment	$1M	(what's needed)
Exit Year	5th Year	(early assumption)
Revenue (5th yr)	$20M	(assumption)
Net Profit (5th yr)	10% = $2M	(assumption)
P/E (industry)	15X	(pick your comp)
Company Value	$30M	(at exit)
Required ROI	10X	(VC model)
Required Valuation	$10M	(of our stake)
% of Company Required	33%	(to net us $10M)
Pre-Money Valuation	$2M	(derived from above)

As you can see from this fourth method, it brings some real world context into things. But it is still pretty simplistic because it only assumes one round of financing and would get pretty complicated as you try to make it track actual reality.

> **The key underlying premise of the Seraf Method is that percentage ownership is the yardstick that allows you to compare a risk-adjusted valuation to market norms.**

Q

So these four common methods have their limitations. When you are negotiating valuations with an entrepreneur, do you use any of these methods, or do you take a different approach?

I know what you are thinking. There has to be a better way. And we think there is. We really don't use these approaches much, favoring our own path which we have developed over time. Our approach continues the tradition of building on everything great that has come before it (with the debt of gratitude acknowledged!), but adds key refinements necessary to make it work reliably in real life. For lack of a better term, let's call it the **Seraf Method**.

In a nutshell, the Seraf Method consists of four simple steps, which we have boiled down into three worksheets and a lookup table.

- The first step is to look up the **exit practicalities** for the company,
- The next step is to think about the **financing requirements**,
- The third step is to look at the current **fund-raising market conditions and current deal details** and
- The fourth and final step is to look up your **valuation on the adjusted "curve"** on the Valuation Look-Up Table.

To help you visualize the method overall, here is a diagram showing the forces at work:

Overview: The Seraf Method

- Exit Reality Adjustments
- Financing Requirements Adjustments
- Current Deal Environment Adjustments
- Valuation Zone

The key underlying premise of the Seraf Method is that percentage ownership is the yardstick that allows you to compare a risk-adjusted valuation to market norms. I think it is important to point out that by using percentages we do not mean to imply that percentage ownership is a particular goal for angels. But rather it is that thinking of it in terms of percentage ownership provides a relative gauge for how a deal valuation stacks up. For venture capitalists, owning a precise percentage is important for reasons of time management and fund returns math (and sometimes, though not often, for control over decision-making - usually that is achieved contractually).

But for angels, this focus on percentage ownership does not really apply to the same extent for several reasons:

- The percentage ownership we are talking about here is ownership by the entire class of investors (e.g. all Series Seed or all Series A investors as a class) and it is split amongst a large group of individuals who will each own a slice of it.

- Angels tend to go into companies at such an early stage that they must make a larger number of lower conviction bets than VCs who are often deploying their biggest chunks of money when companies are more established and starting to go into expansion mode.

- Angels are not hired portfolio managers who need to sit on the board of every investment they make - someone needs to sit on each board, but an angel might only be the board delegate to 1 out of every 10 or 15 of their deals.

So while the Seraf Method revolves around the concept of percentage ownership, it is just a means, not an end. We use percentage ownership because historical market norms allow us to use percentage ownership as a guideline or yardstick.

To use the Seraf Method is pretty simple. Assuming you have done some basic diligence on the company and have a sense of its intended path, you simply buzz through each of the first three worksheets, and the spreadsheet sums up the results and applies that correction to the "curve" embodied in the Valuation Look-Up Table. So without further adieu, let's look at the worksheets.

> For most companies, an IPO is not a realistic possibility. The market for all but the most marquee IPOs is very weak. As a result, only a very tiny fraction of startups will live to see an IPO - the number is way less than 1%.

Seraf Method Worksheet One: Exit Realities

The purpose of Worksheet One is to ballpark the kind of exit that might be possible and use that to create the first set of adjustments to the starting valuation. But to drive home the importance of doing this exit analysis, we first need to set some context about startup exits as a background for using Worksheet One.

Investors can make money in any type of exit, provided the company is capitalized appropriately for that exit. You cannot pour $10M into a company and sell it for $15M and expect to make a good return. In that scenario, even if investors owned 66% of the company, they would still be looking at a 1X. So in thinking about the valuation for a company (and the capital staging plan), you have to start with the realities of what kind of exit the company could reasonably expect to achieve.

For most companies, an IPO is not a realistic possibility. For a lot of reasons (which are beyond the scope of this discussion), the market for all but the most marquee IPOs is very weak. As a result, only a very tiny fraction of startups will live to see an IPO - the number is way less than 1%. Here's the math behind that: conventional wisdom holds that 90% of startups have failed before they reach 5 years old. Even if we conservatively knock that down to a 75% failure rate, of the 25% that do survive, a recent CB Insights Report found that 97% of startups are acquired and 3% did an IPO. So 3% of 25% is 0.75%. And those numbers appear to be going down over a long trend line. In 1997 there were over 7,000 public companies in the US. Now there are less than 4,000. Conclusion: most startups should plan on an exit by M&A.

So how about the deals that do get done? As we previously outlined in detail in our discussion of exit strategy, most exit scenarios can be categorized into one of the following five buckets, whereby the acquirer will either:

- **Buy the Team** - Company has limited if any intrinsic value beyond the knowledge and experience of the team. Acquirer's objective is to hire the people (i.e Acqui-Hire).

- **Buy the Technology** - Company has some Intellectual Property (IP) in addition to the knowledge and experience of the team. Acquirer's objective is to hire the people and obtain control of the IP.

- **Buy the Feature** - Company's technology has some proven capability, but has achieved limited market acceptance. Acquirer is adding a "feature" to its existing product line along with the people who created the IP.

- **Buy the Product** - Company has built a product with early market acceptance and they are nearing product/market fit. Acquirer is buying a product with some traction that they can apply significant sales and marketing resources to and increase growth.

- **Buy the Business** - Company has built a viable, profitable stand-alone business that is centered around one product or a series of closely-related products. Acquirer views this as the purchase of a growth business with the intent of accelerating the growth and increasing profitability.

Most M&A deals are smaller than you might think. Those last two categories (buy the product, or buy the business) are what you are shooting for. If you look at the exit practicalities and you cannot foresee circumstances that could drive it into one of those categories, you are not likely to get a great exit valuation, nor a great return, and you should pay a lower valuation upon your initial investment in the company.

Even if you can find a buyer who will pay a good revenue or EBITDA multiple, you still need meaningful revenue or EBITDA with which to multiply. And before you make huge assumptions on what kind of revenue might be possible, you should sanity check what kind of market share that number would represent. It is unusual to see a small company enter an established market and gobble up 75%+ market share unless they created the market themselves. (Yes, I know Google did it - but I stand by my assertion that it is very rare and associated with massive shifts in technologies and markets).

Assuming you can project decent revenue and margins, a good way to get a sense of whether buyers might be interested, is to look at it through a strategic lens. As we discuss in detail in our discussion of exit strategy, there are numerous scenarios where a large company makes an acquisition, but the following 5 cases are the ones that create the most motivation for acquirers and the most value for the investor:

* A new product that complements a fast growing product line of a large company

* A disruptive product that has the potential to damage a larger company's market position or become difficult to "sell around"

* A new product that fills a newly emerging gap in a big company's product line

* A new product with strategic patents that a buyer cannot risk having fall into a competitor's hands

* A new product that is clearly constrained by lack of sales and would be instantly accretive and profitable in the hands of a larger sales force or sold to an existing customer base.

This list is not exhaustive, but it does cover the outcomes that will produce some of the greatest returns to investors. You will notice that of the original five buckets, the acquisitions of teams, technology and features are not reflected in any of these high value scenarios. So-called "acqui-hires" are a particular issue: they might produce a good financial return for the company founders (especially if the buyer creates a "carve-out" from the proceeds to be paid to the team as an inducement for doing the deal) and therefore be attractive and tempting to the management team, but they rarely turn out to be great returns for the early stage investor.

Other exit factors will include issues like intellectual property that could pose a major threat to a big company, the experience and transferability of the team, market characteristics, competition, timing, other investors, and the current events situation around the company.

The goal of Worksheet One is to walk you through a series of simple questions to help you make "Exit Realities" adjustments to your valuation. When you boil all the relevant concepts down, here is how it looks. For each topic you want to "set the slider" in the right place and tally up your resulting Worksheet One sub-total to be carried forward.

To access an online version of the worksheets, go to:

http://bit.ly/Seraf_Method_Valuations

Valuation Worksheet One: Exit Realities

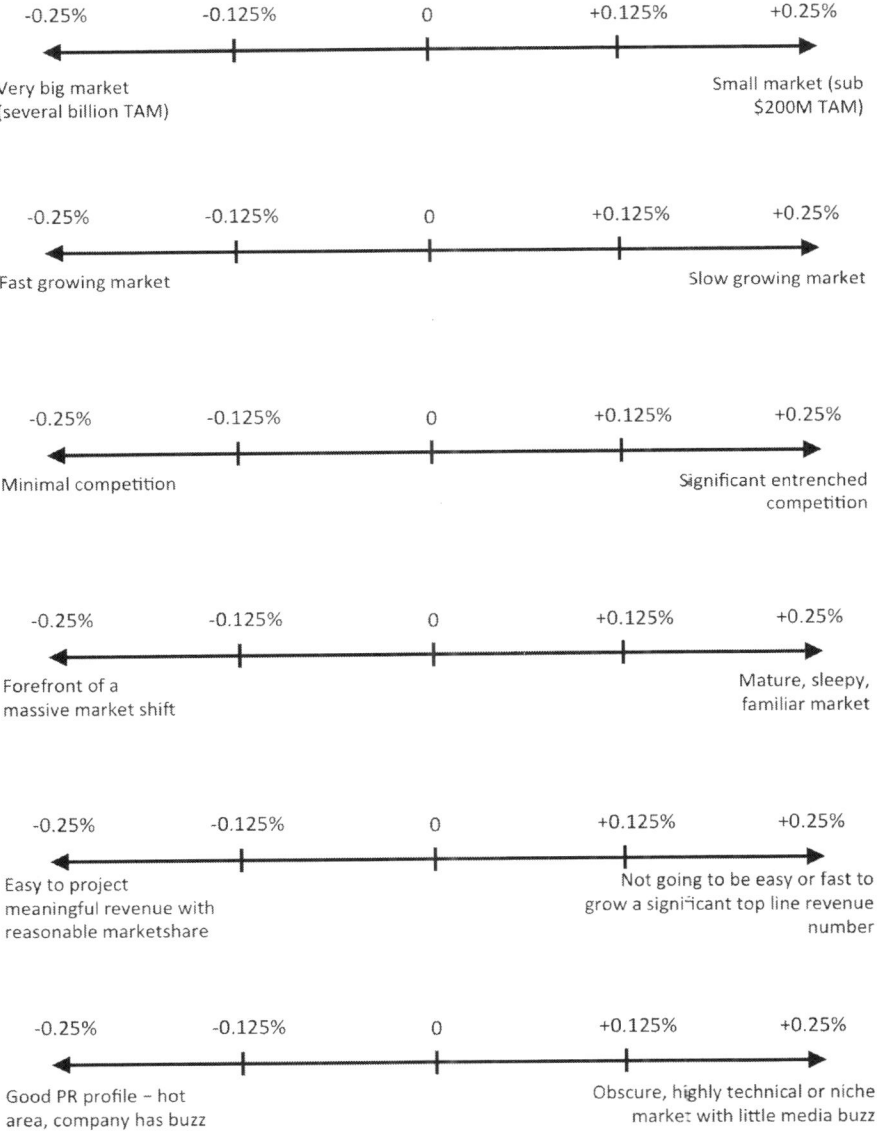

Valuation Worksheet One: Exit Realities (cont.)

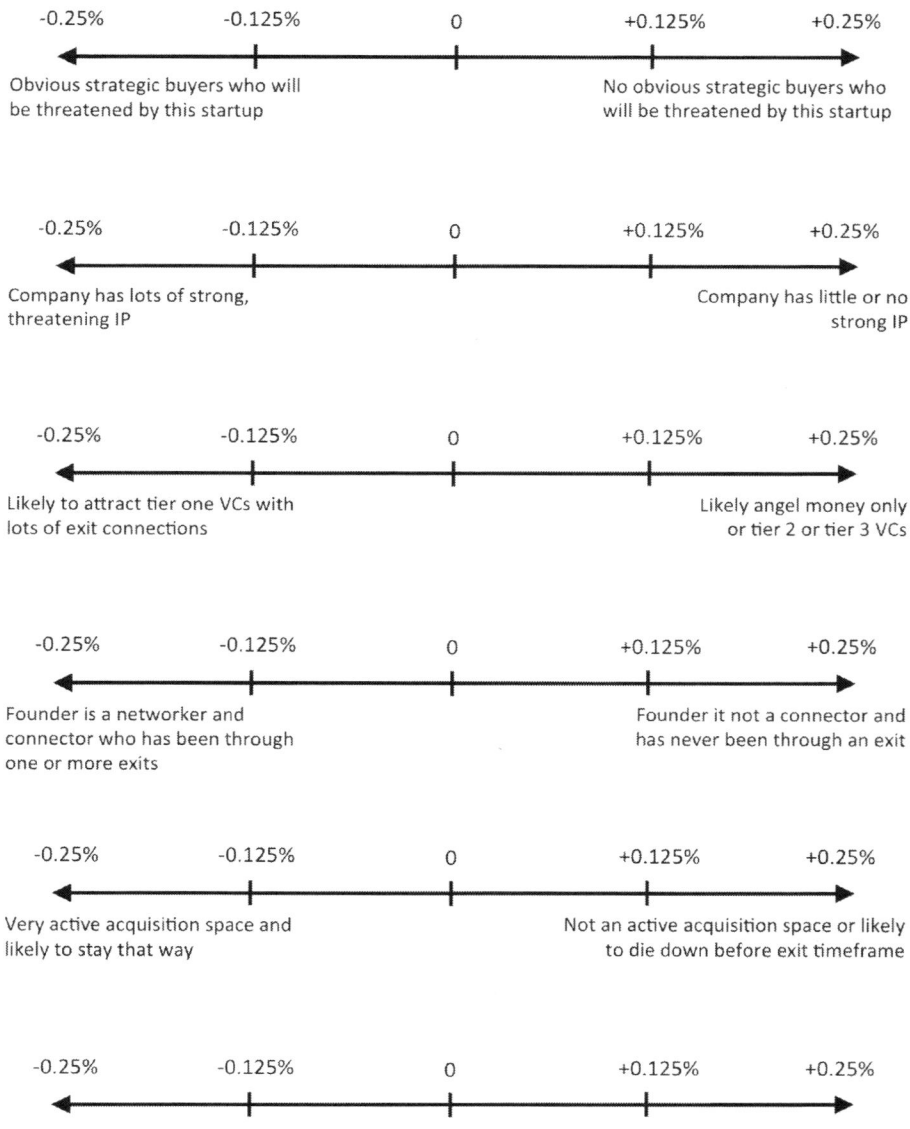

-0.25%	-0.125%	0	+0.125%	+0.25%
Obvious strategic buyers who will be threatened by this startup				No obvious strategic buyers who will be threatened by this startup

-0.25%	-0.125%	0	+0.125%	+0.25%
Company has lots of strong, threatening IP				Company has little or no strong IP

-0.25%	-0.125%	0	+0.125%	+0.25%
Likely to attract tier one VCs with lots of exit connections				Likely angel money only or tier 2 or tier 3 VCs

-0.25%	-0.125%	0	+0.125%	+0.25%
Founder is a networker and connector who has been through one or more exits				Founder it not a connector and has never been through an exit

-0.25%	-0.125%	0	+0.125%	+0.25%
Very active acquisition space and likely to stay that way				Not an active acquisition space or likely to die down before exit timeframe

-0.25%	-0.125%	0	+0.125%	+0.25%
Massive IPO scale very possible				Never going to be a huge company

Seraf Method Worksheet Two: Financing Requirements

The purpose of Worksheet Two is to gauge how much capital it is going to take to move the company to the most logical point of exit and estimate the impact that financing plan should have on the valuation you should pay. This is important to assess in the valuation context because more capital required means more financing risk and more dilution for you, both of which drastically affect your returns. It *should* also enable more growth, but it **definitely does** mean more financing risk and dilution.

Even thriving companies require cash to grow. Let me repeat that for emphasis: growth consumes cash. The reason for that is fairly obvious if you think about it. Take buying a car, for example. Do you pay up front and then have someone go make a car for you? No, walk into a dealership, plunk your money down, and drive out in a car that was already sitting there on the lot. The car company had to design the car, build the factory, purchase the parts, pay the fabricators, and ship the car to the dealer before it could be sold to you. All those things required the seller to burn working capital long before they had your money to defray the costs. If the car company is to grow, it needs to invest working capital. If it is to grow fast, it needs to invest lots of working capital.

> **More capital required means more financing risk and more dilution for you, both of which drastically affect your returns.**

Startups are no different. They need to build a product and figure out how to sell it before they get paid for it. So some additional financing is virtually always required if the company is going to realize its fastest possible growth potential. The terms on which that money comes in will determine whether early investors do well and experience mere arithmetic dilution, or do poorly and experience the feared economic dilution.

The terms on which additional money comes in are driven by two things: (1) how well the company executes and (2) the nature of the company's business model and go-to-market approach.

1. **Execution**: The team's likelihood of executing well is an intangible due diligence question. We strongly believe backing excellent teams is critical to success. So for the purposes of this model, we have to assume you are putting a valuation on a company with a solid team.

2. **Business Model and GTM**: The nature of the business model and planned go-to-market (GTM) is the key factor that will help you ballpark how much additional capital is required. Worksheet Two looks at the key elements of different business models and GTMs and helps you calculate your second set of adjustments - the "Financing Requirements" adjustments - to your valuation. The concepts involved have to do with the cost of going to market, the current state of development, and how quickly the company can convert investments in the business back into cash to help subsidize growth.

If things go according to plan and the company grows wildly, the dilution you experience will be arithmetic (later money comes in on good terms) rather than economic (later money comes in on bad terms). Still, more money required always means more risk and a longer exit timeline. So as a general matter, at the very earliest stages of investing, as a matter of simple economics, you should pay less for deals that have a lot of financing risk and the potential for a lot of dilution. This exercise will help you understand the factors driving this dynamic and create the second set of adjustments to the starting valuation.

Again, for each topic you want to "set the slider" in the right place and tally up your resulting Worksheet Two sub-total to be carried forward. When you boil all the relevant concepts down, here is how it looks.

Valuation Worksheet Two: Financing Requirements

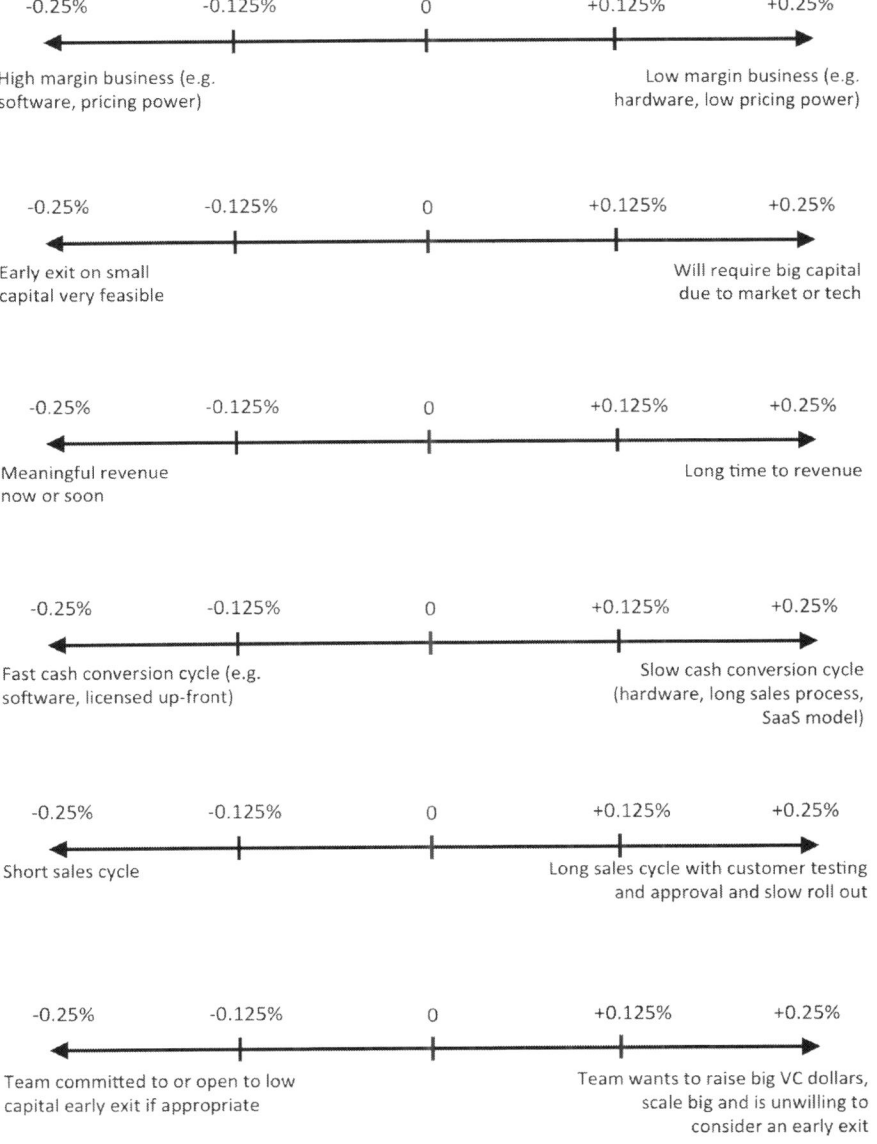

Valuation Worksheet Two: Financing Requirements (cont.)

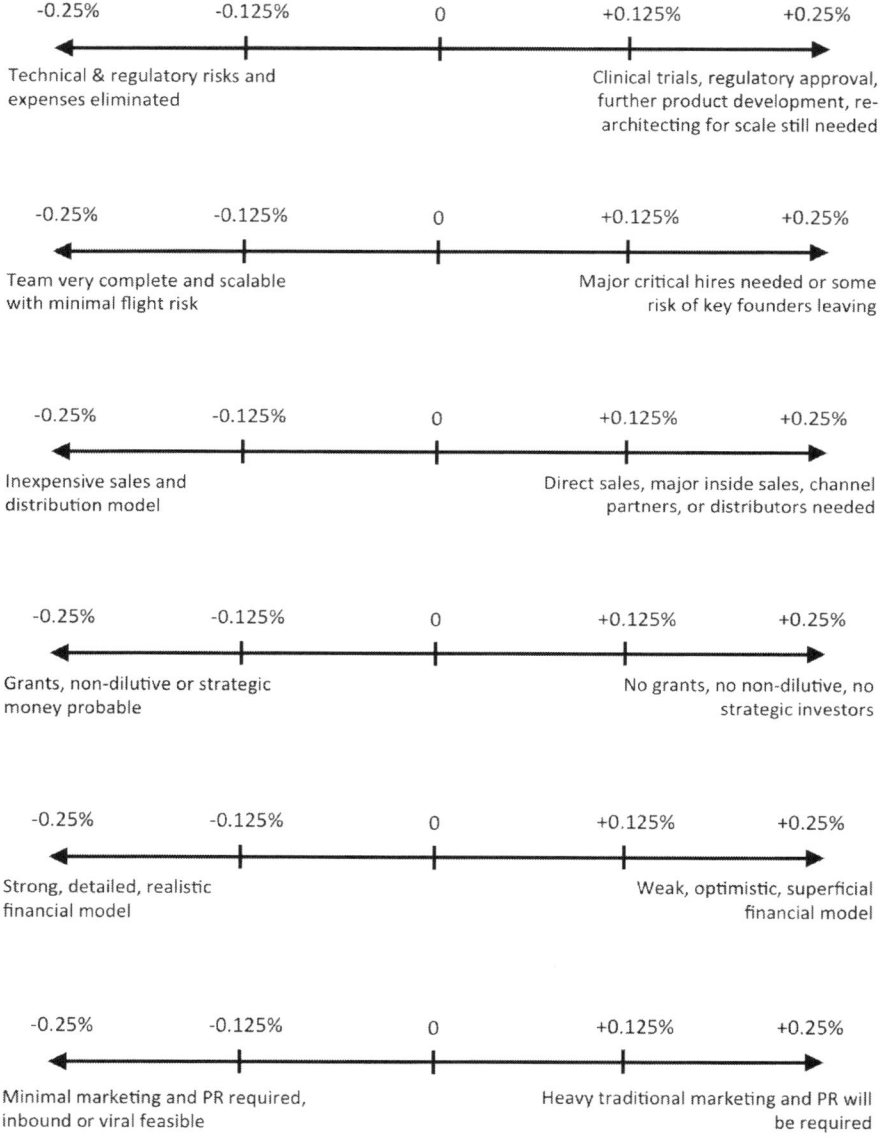

Seraf Method Worksheet Three: Current Deal and Environment

Now we transition from the more macro concepts of the first two worksheets to a more micro set of issues. Worksheet Three helps you assess the relative attractiveness of a particular deal in the real world market context of **your market** at the relevant **moment in time**.

> The reality is that market conditions and the relative attractiveness of a company affect the valuation tremendously.

How many times have you heard someone explain away a deal that couldn't raise money, or a deal that raised at a seemingly crazy high valuation as "a function of the market" or "what the market will bear"? Investors may like to think we have valuation completely down to a science, but the reality is that market conditions and the **relative** attractiveness of a company affect the valuation tremendously.

For example, if a hot new company comes along with:

- A terrific pitch,
- A dynamic team,
- Ready to go in an obvious market,
- A deal with good terms, and
- A great board and advisors,

they are going to benefit from a higher valuation.

But if a company has:

- A team that has been muddling around trying to fundraise for a while,
- Significant technical or regulatory risk still remaining,
- No revenue or demonstrable traction,
- Unusual or unattractive deal terms,

they are going to suffer in terms of valuation.

Another factor to consider: the presence or threat of a possible alternative term sheet can have a significant impact on the valuation a deal settles around.

The point is that deals happen in a market. The market conditions and the relative attractiveness of the opportunity are the final set of adjustments you need to make in Worksheet Three before you are ready to settle on your final valuation in the Valuation Look-Up Table.

On the following page is what Worksheet Three looks like. As with the other two, you need to set the sliders to reflect how the deal scores on the key issues and carry that subtotal forward.

Valuation Worksheet Three: Current Deal & Environment

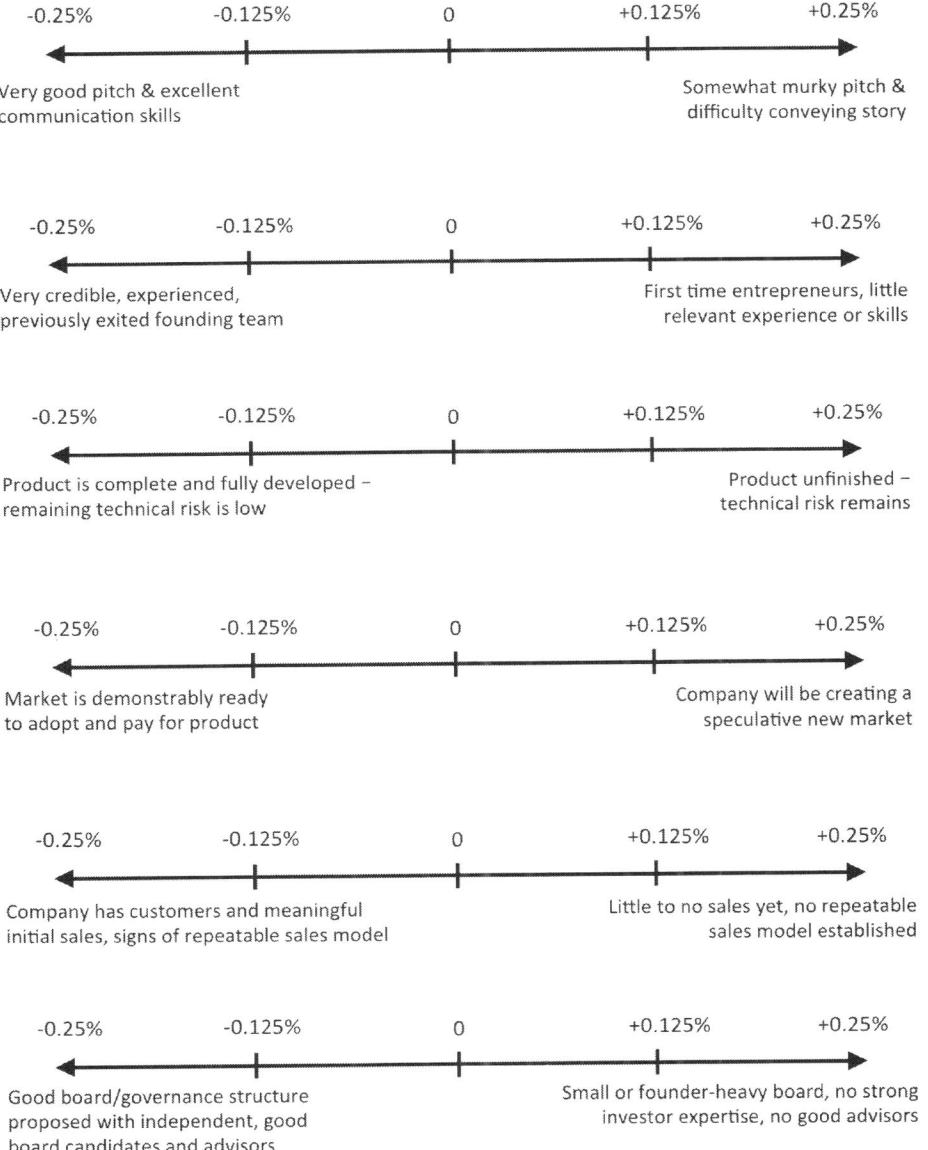

```
    -0.25%      -0.125%         0        +0.125%       +0.25%
      <─────────────┼─────────────┼─────────────┼─────────────>
Very good pitch & excellent                   Somewhat murky pitch &
communication skills                          difficulty conveying story


    -0.25%      -0.125%         0        +0.125%       +0.25%
      <─────────────┼─────────────┼─────────────┼─────────────>
Very credible, experienced,                   First time entrepreneurs, little
previously exited founding team               relevant experience or skills


    -0.25%      -0.125%         0        +0.125%       +0.25%
      <─────────────┼─────────────┼─────────────┼─────────────>
Product is complete and fully developed –     Product unfinished –
remaining technical risk is low               technical risk remains


    -0.25%      -0.125%         0        +0.125%       +0.25%
      <─────────────┼─────────────┼─────────────┼─────────────>
Market is demonstrably ready                  Company will be creating a
to adopt and pay for product                  speculative new market


    -0.25%      -0.125%         0        +0.125%       +0.25%
      <─────────────┼─────────────┼─────────────┼─────────────>
Company has customers and meaningful          Little to no sales yet, no repeatable
initial sales, signs of repeatable sales model    sales model established


    -0.25%      -0.125%         0        +0.125%       +0.25%
      <─────────────┼─────────────┼─────────────┼─────────────>
Good board/governance structure               Small or founder-heavy board, no strong
proposed with independent, good               investor expertise, no good advisors
board candidates and advisors
```

Valuation Worksheet Three: Current Deal & Environment (cont.)

```
-0.25%      -0.125%        0        +0.125%      +0.25%
<----------------+---------+----------+------------>
Company fund-raising just started –          Company has been fund-raising for a
fresh, hot, has momentum                     while, somewhat stale, over-shopped
```

```
-0.25%      -0.125%        0        +0.125%      +0.25%
<----------------+---------+----------+------------>
Attractive deal structure (priced            Investor unfriendly terms, convertible
rather than note), good deal terms           debt, key protections missing
```

```
-0.25%      -0.125%        0        +0.125%      +0.25%
<----------------+---------+----------+------------>
Investor interest building, syndication      No soft-circles, big round size, no
feasible, manageable round size, easy        syndicate, holiday or summer season
time of year to raise
```

```
-0.25%      -0.125%        0        +0.125%      +0.25%
<----------------+---------+----------+------------>
Strong credible deal lead with good          No clear strong deal lead, no diligence
written shareable diligence report           reports, "party round" with no one in
                                             charge
```

```
-0.25%      -0.125%        0        +0.125%      +0.25%
<----------------+---------+----------+------------>
Other competitive investors circling,        No competing term sheets
threat of alternative termsheet              likely or foreseeable
```

Seraf Method: Valuation Look-Up Table

For our final step, we bring it all together and apply our adjustments to a valuation starting point. As the Berkus, Payne and Risk Factor Methods illustrate, you have to start somewhere. But, in our view, an approach based on picking an arbitrary one-size-fits-all number does not drive a good enough result. To find a reasonable starting point, you have to take into account historical market norms and the size of your particular deal. Market statistics can help with that. Thinking of it in terms of percentage ownership is a good yardstick. In our experience, different size rounds tend to be associated with different ownership percentages.

When you look at the tens of thousands of early stage deals which were financed each year over the last few decades, in the vast majority of initial rounds (i.e. "professional" first rounds, not informal friends & family rounds), investors ended up acquiring between 10% and 40% of the company on a post-money basis. And when you remove outliers and special circumstances, the reality is that virtually all mainstream deals end up with investors acquiring something in the range of 15-30% of the company as a result of the round.

In our experience, where in that range of percentage ownership a given deal starts out depends in very large part on factors which tie back in one way or another to future financing risk - how much more money will have to be raised in future rounds. For example: if the company is raising a small amount of money, it won't get very far on this money, and will definitely need to go back out into the market and raise more money fairly quickly. In that scenario, investors are going to want a valuation which results in ownership towards the 30% end of the prevailing range because they know there is a risk that the money may not come, and even if it does come, the terms may not be attractive enough to protect from economic dilution.

However, if the company is raising a really good chunk of money and can presumably go a bit longer and accomplish a lot more, then chances are decent that they will be able to raise future money on their own more favorable terms with less dilution for existing investors. In that case, investors might be more willing to pay a higher valuation that pushes them farther down toward the 15% end of the spectrum.

Envisioned as a sliding scale, prevailing ownerships and valuations would look like the chart below, with round size on the horizontal axis, post-money on the vertical axis, and a real-world pre-money valuation along the diagonal scale.

As you can see from the chart, the valuation line is not a 45 degree angle. It is flattened out a bit because there is a sliding scale of percentage ownership. With the smaller round sizes, the percentage ownership tends to be greater to reflect real world realities and perceived risks. As the company contemplates larger round sizes, the company has more resources to apply to growth, so risk goes down and the effective percentage ownership required also goes down. (It also has more investor

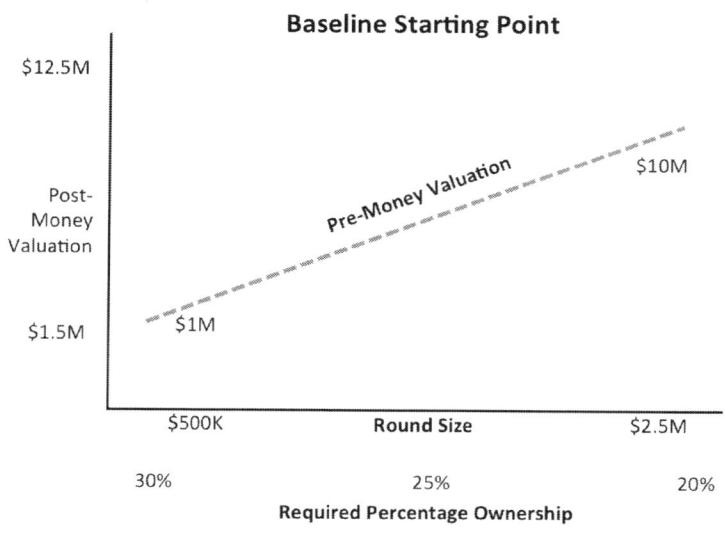

interest to work with to help fill that larger round, which helps prop up the valuation.)

By using this type of sliding scale, you are adjusting for market realities and prevailing norms from the many deals which get done each year. This table is designed to provide a pre-adjustment starting point for the core 20%-25% band where most of the mainstream deals are going to branch out from, and it assumes some of the most common early stage round sizes. However, as you adjust away from the starting point using your data and responses from the first three worksheets, the adjustments you make to your percentages should allow you to cover the entire spectrum of deals that have workable founder and investor economics.

Since no deal is perfect, and all have some strengths and some weaknesses, the expectation is that many of the worksheet adjustments will cancel each other out. In fact, if you find the adjustments are all trending predominantly in one direction, and you are moving toward the extremes of the 10-40% range, that should be a major red flag. In those kinds of deals, investors should proceed with some real caution, and perhaps consider doing some additional diligence. Investors at those extremes may either be seriously overpaying for something that just is not as good as it seems, or may be entering a deal with a beaten-down team that will not be retaining enough ownership to be motivated when the going gets tough.

> **Since no deal is perfect, and all have some strengths and some weaknesses, the expectation is that many of the worksheet adjustments will cancel each other out. In fact, if you find the adjustments are all trending predominantly in one direction, and you are moving toward the extremes of the 10-40% range, that should be a major red flag. In those kinds of deals, investors should proceed with some real caution, and perhaps consider doing some additional diligence.**

To utilize the Valuation Look-Up Table and obtain your final valuation adjustment, the spreadsheet carries forward your net adjustment from the first three worksheets and applies them to the Valuation Look-Up Table. For example, if you found a company that looked really good, the first three worksheets might net out to an adjustment **downward** of half a percentage point in the amount investors feel they need to own, with a resulting increase in the valuation investors are willing to pay. Here is an example of that:

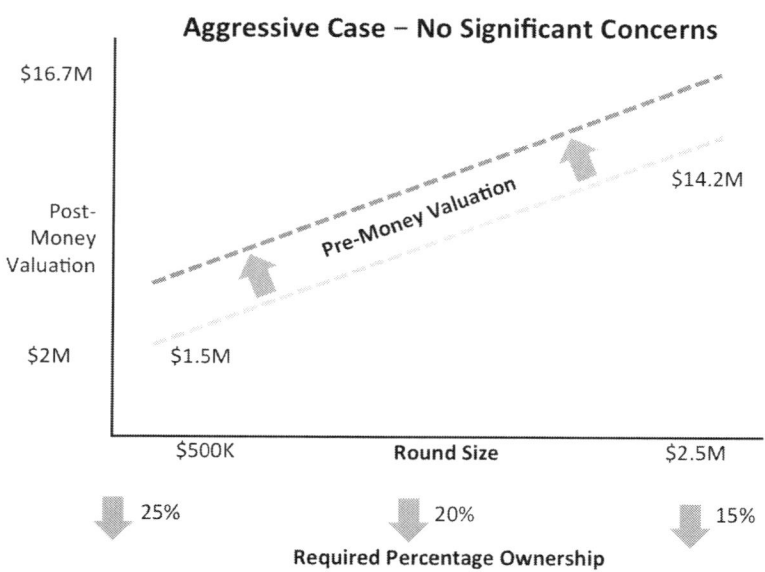

By contrast, if you found an example of a company that raised a few more concerns, the first three worksheets might total out to a half a percentage point increase in the amount you'd need to own, with the resulting decrease in valuation investors would be willing to pay. Here is an example of what that looks like in the chart below.

To download and tweak the assumptions in your own copy of the Worksheet and Look-Up Table package that comprises the Seraf Method, go here: http://bit.ly/Seraf_Method_Valuations.

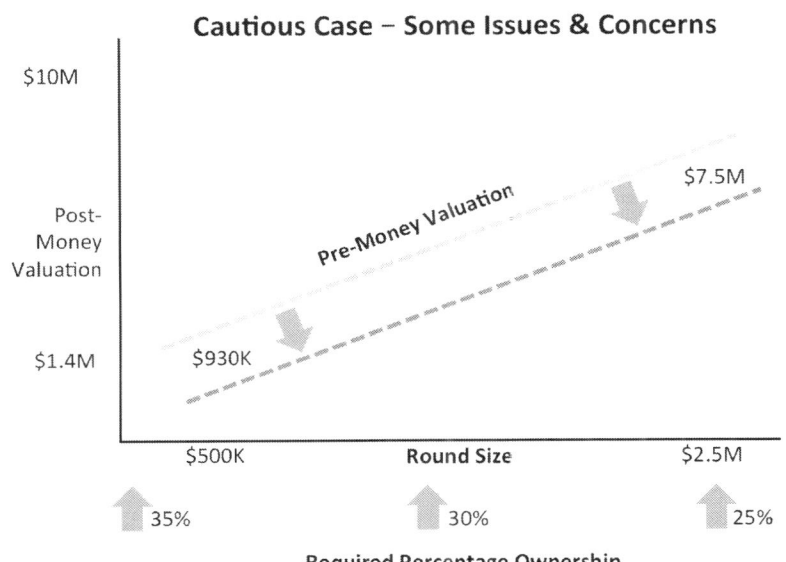

To visualize it in terms of the original circles diagram, here is the starting point:

By contrast, here is a deal where you feel less good about the risk level and decide you must adjust the required percentage ownership up on your worksheets:

And finally, here is a visualization of a deal where the perceived risk level is low and you feel it is acceptable to pay a higher valuation:

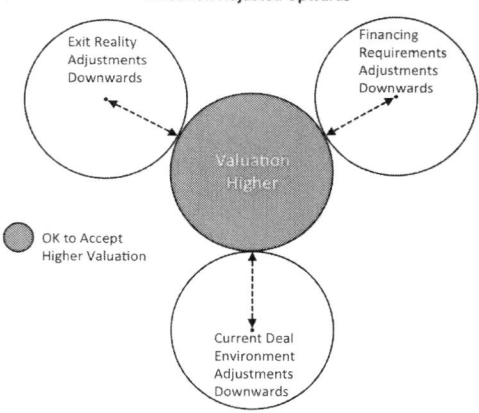

How to Combine the Worksheets: The Seraf Method

Using the worksheets is fairly simple. Once you have done some basic diligence about the opportunity and are comfortable you are dealing with a solid team, you download a copy of the Worksheet and Look-Up Table package that comprises the Seraf Method (http://bit.ly/Seraf_Method_Valuations) and simply work through the drop-downs on each worksheet tab in whatever order you like and the spreadsheet carries your adjustment factor forward to the Valuation Look-Up Table on the fourth tab.

So, for example, Worksheet One might result in a +0.25 percentage point increase, Worksheet Two might be +0.5 and Worksheet Three might be -0.25, resulting in a total adjustment of percentage required at +0.5. The spreadsheet carries that combined adjustment forward to tab four/Valuation Look-Up Table, and adds the adjustment in to get the new "curve," and you look up your round size in the resulting table to find the suggested pre-money valuation.

Investing at the right valuation is vitally important for both the entrepreneur and the investor. If you come in at too low of a valuation the founder economics and incentives can be destroyed. And if you come in at too high a valuation, you may have difficulty filling the round or sustaining the post-money valuation. And even if the company does survive, your returns will be far lower than they should be for the risk and illiquidity undertaken.

As you can see from these worksheets, there are many different concepts involved in arriving at a good risk-adjusted valuation - the exit realities, the financing plan and the circumstances around the deal itself. We have tried to put in the effort to boil our learning and experience down into a simple tool that will allow you to make sophisticated adjustments more easily. By working through the Seraf Method you should have a very quick, organized and, most importantly, realistic and reliable method for coming up with a valuation that properly captures your deal's true value.

Q

How do you handle the valuation discussion with the entrepreneur?

This can be a tricky discussion, but it helps if you start with the right mindset:

- Have some humility and respect for the entrepreneur and don't approach it with a superior "I hold all the money and all the cards" attitude.

- Have some empathy and recognize that this is a stressful situation for them to be in and an area where they might have much less comfort or working knowledge than you do.

- Treat it like you are trying to form a partnership of equals that is fair to both sides and will work for the long term good of the company.

- Think of it more as an opportunity to **educate** than to **negotiate**.

If you have that mindset, you are going to go a long way toward being successful right from the start. You can begin your conversation by talking about shared goals: getting a good round done quickly that is fair to both sides and allow them to get back to running the business.

Once you establish that shared goal, you can talk about what you think it will take to bring the investors in, and why you think that. This is your chance to educate. It is not about beating an entrepreneur down so much as:

- Helping them see the deal through the eyes of an investor and

- Helping them understand the implications of post-money valuation in terms of staging capital and getting ahead of yourself on the valuation curve.

- Sharing a waterfall analysis model which illustrates the economic impact of valuation changes.

In a typical deal, a relatively small change in valuation might have a big impact on investor appetite, but a much smaller impact on the entrepreneur's outcome. For example, in the Appendix on Capitalization Tables we discuss how the difference between a $3.6M pre-money and a $4M pre-money works out to about a 5% difference in outcome for the founders, using reasonable assumptions.

Q

If we are still far apart on price, can't you just fix it with deal terms?

When you still cannot bridge that gap, you may be tempted to try and compensate for not getting the valuation you want by changing other terms in the deal. My advice is to resist that temptation and tread very carefully here. With early stage term sheets, your goal, as much as possible, should be to keep the terms as vanilla as you can. Any funky terms you help yourself to will inevitably end up either being friction which hampers bringing later money in, or terms insisted on by later much bigger rounds, or both. In other words, by trying to help yourself a little bit, you can actually end up hurting yourself a lot.

> **With early stage term sheets, your goal, as much as possible, should be to keep the terms as vanilla as you can.**

The one exception to this might be with special business terms designed to address very specific business risks. For example, if you fear a product will not ship on time or revenue targets may not be hit, you can address that concern with incentive compensation for the team, or other kinds of carrot/stick tools such as operating or governance covenants the board can administer. That kind of term makes good sense and is specific to the business risks in a way that, say, helping yourself to a 2X liquidation preference wouldn't be.

Incentivizing management is totally legitimate and understandable to later investors if it is even visible or an issue at all. By contrast, an off market term like a multiple liquidation preference would be a disaster for your deal long term.

Options in particular can be a very powerful tool for use in this context. Granting options to the management team as part of a deal can be a very powerful way of both managing their dilution concerns, and also incentivizing their future performance. Options can also be used as a crude way of creating an adjustable purchase price for situations where the revenue path may vary widely. For example, we have done deals where a large special pool is created where management would vest grants if certain sales targets were hit. It worked very well as a simple mechanism for bridging a gap where we wanted to pay a lower valuation for fear the revenue forecast would not be hit, and management wanted a higher valuation because they believed in their huge forecast. The way the mechanism worked, if management hit the targets, they would vest big option grants which would have the result of raising the effective deal valuation, whereas if they did not, the lower valuation would remain.

Valuation discussions are hard, and they can be very fraught with emotion. But with the right attitude, some listening and educational skills, the right tools, and a little creativity, you can work your way through this process and forge not only a great deal for all involved, but also a great relationship with your new partner, the CEO.

Have you run into situations over the years with poorly valued companies?

I might not have made every dumb investor mistake in the book, but I've certainly made a few. Three examples where I wish I had thought twice come to mind.

Investing in a hot deal with a large pre-money valuation: This might be the most common mistake early stage investors make. You are introduced to a rock star entrepreneur at a Demo Day event. She just finished a great pitch to a huge live audience and everyone wants in on the deal. Investor demand means the round will be oversubscribed. So guess what? The deal ends up being overpriced. In situations like this, it's not unusual for the company's valuation to be 2X or 3X what it would be in normal circumstances. Even if the company does well and has a nice exit, your return probably won't be worth the risk you took.

Investing in an uncapped convertible note: One of the very first investments I made was in a young entrepreneur in Boston. I liked him a lot and thought the product idea was solid. He was totally broke and was trying to raise a tiny round on the simplest and cheapest possible terms. I wanted to help him out. Since I was new to the angel investing world, I didn't fully understand the ramifications of investing in an uncapped convertible note. Shortly after I made the investment, the entrepreneur moved his company to San Francisco and raised a small amount of money at a $20M pre-money valuation. My note converted to stock at that valuation. Ultimately, the company was acquired, and I doubled my money. Not a bad return on my investment, but if I had insisted on a reasonable cap to the note (say $4M), my return would have been 10X not 2X!

> Valuation discussions are hard, and they can be very fraught with emotion. But with the right attitude, some listening and educational skills, the right tools, and a little creativity, you can work your way through this process and forge not only a great deal for all involved, but also a great relationship with your new partner, the CEO.

This third example might be a little ironic in a chapter about valuation disciplines, but one of the biggest mistakes I ever made or an angel can make, is **passing on a great entrepreneur because the valuation was a bit high**: Ham likes to remind me of this mistake every once in a while just to get my goat! A small group of Launchpad members decided to invest in a medical device company. It was a very early stage company founded by a proven entrepreneur. Given the stage of the company, I thought the valuation was about 25% too high. So I took a pass on the investment. Fast forward to a few years later and the company is doing incredibly well. They are on track for a grand slam exit. I sure wish I hadn't passed on that one. If I had understood the concepts underlying the Seraf Method better, I would have made all the downward adjustments to the sliders and had the perspective to recognize that valuation for what it was: a good deal!

Chapter 3

Beating the Odds: Startup Pathways to Success

As an active angel investor in the Boston tech sector, I witnessed many paths to a successful return on my invested capital. Sometimes the path is short and sweet. Other times the path is long and convoluted, but ultimately leads to a happy ending. I subscribe to the belief that as an angel investor I should be open to a variety of investment opportunities as I build a successful, early stage company portfolio.

Anyone who has been around the tech startup world is certainly familiar with some of the big successes in venture capital. Companies such as Google, Amazon and Facebook made billions for the investors at Kleiner Perkins, Sequoia and Accel. Such multi-billion dollar exits are the fuel that drives the venture capital industry. But, according to industry analysts such as CB Insights, these unicorn exits represent a tiny percentage of the successful exits in tech.

> **You can make money in any kind of exit as long as the staging of capital and the valuations at which it went in are appropriate for the exit type.**

If you are like me, you make most, if not all of your angel investments in your local area. Here in Boston, we've had many billion dollar exits over the past 50 years, but they represent a tiny fraction of the total number of exits. Unless you live in Silicon Valley during a boom cycle, you are lucky if there are more than one or two of these unicorn exits over a ten year time frame.

So, is it possible for an angel to make venture capital returns (e.g. 25+% IRR sustained over many years) if you don't have access to a steady stream of potential unicorn-sized exits? The answer is absolutely yes, as long as you understand how to properly finance a company from its earliest days all the way through to its exit. As many people have heard us say, "You can make money in any kind of exit as long as the staging of capital and the valuations at which it went in are appropriate for the exit type."

To help show how this works, we are going to give some examples using numbers. To ensure the math in this article is illuminating, we are going to assume you are an early stage investor who is not investing from a large fund and does not have unlimited capital to put into every deal. Maybe you are an angel investing $500K, or perhaps, a professional angel willing to invest $20M in startups. With that in mind, let's ask Ham how he builds his portfolio with a mixture of small, medium and large potential companies.

Q

Ham, what are the primary pathways to an exit for a successful angel investment?

I like to break down the potential exits in my portfolio into four separate categories. The categories include:

- Early Exit
- Dividend, Royalty or Buy-back
- Large Acquisition
- Successful IPO

It's important to point out that your investment returns (and IRR) can vary significantly under each scenario. For example, in an early exit, you might be lucky to get twice your money back if the acquiring company is just interested in hiring the founders and their team. On the other hand, if the acquiring company needs the core technology for strategic reasons, you could be looking at a 10x or greater return.

No matter which path the company ultimately heads down, it cannot be left to random chance. Building a solid exit strategy in the early days of the company, and refining that strategy as time progresses, is crucial for driving the optimal investment outcome because capitalization decisions need to be calibrated to match likely exit scenarios.

Q

What are some of the successful financing strategies you've seen companies employ to help optimize the investment outcome?

Raising the right amount of financing for a successful exit takes a lot of forethought. Having a solid understanding of your long-term capital requirements is crucial planning for all the company shareholders (e.g. management and investors.) Over-capitalize the business and your returns will be sub-optimal. Under-capitalize the business and you might never reach an exit because you fail to hit your escape velocity.

> **Raising the right amount of financing for a successful exit takes a lot of forethought. Having a solid understanding of your long-term capital requirements is crucial planning for all the company shareholders.**

Let's illustrate this by outlining four examples of how this works so I can discuss the strategies that should be employed to help drive a successful outcome.

Example One

Let's begin with a relatively capital-efficient software business. And let's make a few assumptions: 1) at the time of your initial investment the company bootstrapped its way to shipping product and a small amount of initial revenue, and 2) the product provides real value to an already existing market of decent size that is dominated by 3 or 4 large software companies, limiting likely market share to something less than half. Based on these assumptions, and historical norms, the most likely successful outcome for our company is an acquisition in a best-case 5 year timeframe with a target exit price in the $20M to $40M range.

Now, let's overlay some investor math to see whether you can achieve your investment objectives as an angel investor. Given the risk, illiquidity, time and effort, you need to be able to model a possible 10X return for all your investments (if you cannot model that level of return at the honeymoon stage, you are exceedingly unlikely to see an acceptable multiple once the plan has collided with reality). We need to make one more assumption before we can complete this exercise. To make the math easier let's generously assume that valuations have been reasonable and after all the rounds of financing the investors own 50% of the company. Based on our target acquisition price $20M to $40M, the investors end up with return capital somewhere between $10M and $20M. For the investors to achieve a 10X return, the total amount of equity capital raised needs to be in the $1M to $2M range. That's not a lot, but in our very simple example that's what it needs to be! And that is assuming investors hold 50% - they might end up with less.

It's not too hard to put together a spreadsheet (see the Appendix on Capitalization Tables) to model the financing and exit plan for a company. I encourage all investors to take the time to understand this math and make sure the CEO does as well!

Example Two

My first example was pretty basic, but with good financial discipline and some significant customer revenue, great CEOs can achieve those results. But what about a more complex example? Our second example is in a technology company that's an early entrant in a brand new market. Let's make the following assumptions: 1) at the time of your initial investment the company built a prototype using non-dilutive financing from government grants, and 2) they've built a product that addresses the needs of a potentially very large market.

Based on these assumptions, you'll tend to see two different exit paths. The first path is a relatively capital efficient path that results in the company being acquired in a few years as big companies start to realize the potential size of the new market and choose to make strategic acquisitions to establish a market presence. These early exits can range all over the place, but are typically at the $20M to $100M scale. Performing similar math to our first example, the investors can expect a 10X or greater return if the company raises between $1M and $5M.

Example Three

But what if the company decides to turn down those lucrative early offers and tries to go big? What happens then? Well, first off, the company will need to raise a significant amount of capital in order to build a much bigger company. In scenarios like this, it's not unusual for companies to raise $10M to $50M, or more over 2, 3 even 4 rounds of financing. Now, in addition to the much-extended time scale associated with building a large company, the exit math also becomes much more complicated. That spreadsheet I described above has a few more rows and columns! A typical scenario results in the early investors having their ownership position reduced by subsequent rounds to around 10% for the $2M they invested in the early days. Once that level of dilution is factored in, for the angels to achieve their 10X return, the company must be acquired for more than $200M. Large exits at that size do happen, but the bigger the exit, the less frequently it occurs, so the odds of success for the investors are much, much lower. And, don't forget the impact that this will have on your IRR. That 10X return is now extended out by 5 or more years on top of the typical 5 years. Your exit multiple might be the same in both cases, but your IRR has dropped significantly!

> Large exits over $200M do happen, but the bigger the exit, the less frequently it occurs, so the odds of success for the investors are much, much lower.

Example Four

What happens if, as all too commonly occurs, the company and its investors pick the worst of both models? What if the company raises lots of money and tries to go big, but ends up lucky to get a $40M exit? Well, if the angel investors put in $2M but were diluted down to 10%, they would be looking at about a 2X return. Given the ten year time horizon, that is about a 7% IRR! That is a horrible outcome given the amount of risk and illiquidity undertaken, especially if you subtract from that return what the money would have done in a broad stock market index over the same period. How did that dismal return occur? The capitalization strategy did not match the exit realities. The company loaded up on tons of equity capital but was lucky to get a low single digit multiple of revenue for an average price.

Q

As an early stage, angel investor, what happens to my ownership position in the company as each new round of venturing financing occurs?

It shouldn't come as much of a surprise to investors that their original ownership percentage shrinks every time additional equity capital is raised by the company. That said, it's helpful to apply some real numbers based on actual data to give investors a better sense for what is going on.

In 2016, CapShare analyzed over 5,000 cap tables from private companies who use their Cap Table Management software. Their research highlighted some key insights that are highly relevant to both management and investors. Starting with the Series Seed round and going through the Series A, B, C and D rounds, the average dilution for all stockholders was approximately twenty to twenty-five percent at each round. That means by the Series D round, the founder's ownership share was reduced from 100% to a range of 11 to 17%.

For the angels who participated in the Seed Round, they can expect their ownership percentage to decline at a similar rate. So if, as an individual angel, you start off personally owning 1% of the company after the Series Seed, you will be down to less than 0.4% at the Series D round. You can avoid this dilution by exercising your pro-rata rights and continuing to invest in the company, but that might require more capital than you plan on investing in just this one company.

One important side note on this topic. As Christopher likes to point out, there is a big difference between "arithmetic dilution" and "economic dilution." Just because your percentage ownership is going down, does not mean the value of your holding is. Although your ownership percentage might decrease with each round of financing, the value of your position will move based on a more important variable -- the post-money valuation of the company. So as long as the company is making progress and the value of the business increases, you should expect your investment to increase in value over time even though your ownership percentage is shrinking. You are arithmetically diluted, but not economically diluted. Your slice of the pie is smaller, but the increase in the worth of the overall pie more than makes up for it.

> There is a big difference between "arithmetic dilution" and "economic dilution." Just because your percentage ownership is going down, does not mean the value of your holding is.

Q

Can you provide us with some data on the range of acquisition price for a technology company?

There are many great sources of data from the technology investment world, including Investment Banks (e.g. Goldman Sachs, JP Morgan), Accounting Firms (e.g. PwC Moneytree) and Research Firms (e.g. CB Insights, Pitchbook, Crunchbase). If you are the type of investor who likes to dig into data, I encourage you to go online and access the reports from these organizations. Many of these firms have blogs and newsletters that you can subscribe to in order to stay on top of industry financial trends.

One of the more comprehensive research organizations for tracking technology company exits is CB Insights. As of this writing, the most recent report on exits was their 2016 Global Tech Exits Report. This report analyzes the results from 3,358 exits in 2016. Out of this cohort of companies, 97% exited through an acquisition and 3% made it all the way to an IPO.

The breakdown for exit size is as follows:

- Under $50M   54%
- $50M and $100M   13%
- $100M and $200M   13%
- $200M and $300M   7%
- $300M and $400M   4%
- $400M and $500M   1%
- $500M and $1B   6%
- Greater than $1B   4%

As you can see from this breakdown, 80% of exits they tracked are for less than $200M. For investors looking to achieve a 10x return, the company has to raise quite a bit less than $20M in equity over its financing history.

Please note that this report from CB Insights does not cover all exits that happened in 2016. In fact, it is probably overly rosy in its outlook. It's impossible to track every deal that occurs throughout the year,

largely due to the lack of publicity and small transaction size for many deals. Smaller deals are far more likely to go untracked. If you were to factor in these transactions, the percentage of exits that are less than $50M in size would likely be much larger than the 54% indicated by the CB Insights report.

Q

Why aren't VCs interested in investing in companies that will, in a best case scenario, end up selling for around $50M?

Ultimately, the answer to this question comes down to an issue related to the amount of capital that a typical VC fund needs to invest. The best way to answer this question is to do a little bit of math, so here we go again:

- Let's say that the VC Firm is small and has a $100M fund

- For the fund to be considered a reasonable success by industry metrics, it must return at least $250M to the fund's limited partners (2.5x capital invested)

- The fund makes investments into 15 companies

- On average, each company will receive $6M in equity capital from the fund

- With this $6M investment, the fund will own 20% of each company

- A top performing fund will end up with ⅓ failures, ⅓ returning invested capital and ⅓ large successes

- That means the fund will return approximately zero from one third, $30M of capital from another third, which means ⅔ of its portfolio returns just 30% of the fund.

- So the remaining 5 companies need to return $220M in total to make the fund successful

- That means, on average, each of the 5 remaining companies has to return $44M to the fund

- If the fund owns 20% of each company, to end up with a $44M return, the exit size for each company has to be over $200M

> **If a VC can only model a $50M exit as a best case scenario for a company, they are looking at a return of $10M to the fund. It's hard to justify the time and effort of putting such a small investment into their fund.**

As we have just agreed, $200M exits are just not that common. So the VC needs to bank on the fact that one of its companies will be a $1B exit. And that is not going to happen if you are focusing on $50M opportunities. Although this may be a gross oversimplification of the equity investment approach by a VC fund, it does highlight the importance of exit size to the ultimate financial success of the fund. If a VC can only model a $50M exit as a best case scenario for a company, they are looking at a return of $10M to the fund. It's hard to justify the time and effort of putting such a small investment into their fund.

Angels and very small funds (i.e. funds with less than $25M in capital) do have the ability to make profitable investments into smaller opportunities. As long as the total amount of equity capital raised by one of these small exit opportunity companies is less than $3M, the math can work out well for this type of investor. So, I am not surprised when I hear that VC firms make 3,000 to 4,000 investments in a typical year and angels make 50,000 to 70,000 investments per year. There are so many more small exits that occur each year that ultimately will end up making a great return for angel investors.

Chapter 4

Mule Team: Building a Startup Portfolio That Will Get You There

When I began making angel investments almost twenty years ago, I had no concept of what it meant to build a portfolio of early stage tech company investments. It wasn't because I lacked financial savvy. I considered myself a fairly knowledgeable investor in the public markets. I understood key investing concepts like portfolio diversification, risk-adjusted investment return, market capitalization, and staging capital. However, I didn't have a grasp on those terms in the context of making angel investments.

For the first few years as an active angel, I invested in a variety of companies. I didn't put any thought into building a diverse portfolio that would result in solid financial returns given the risk I was taking investing in illiquid, high risk, early stage technology stocks.

Lucky for me, I live in Boston where there is a vibrant investment community of VCs and public company fund managers. A number of these investors were willing to help me understand the importance of thinking about my investments working together in the context of a portfolio of investments instead of just a random collection of companies. It took many conversations, a lot of study, and a bunch of reflecting on experiences to wrap my head around this approach to angel investing.

When I first met Christopher in 2009, I passed along some of my well-earned knowledge of angel investing to help him shape his portfolio. Since that time we have refined our thinking across investments in dozens and dozens of companies and continued conversations with our financially experienced colleagues in Boston and around the US. Our experience has led us to believe that for any angel investor to have long term success investing in early stage companies, they must construct a well-thought-out portfolio.

Q

Christopher, what are some of the key investing concepts an angel investor needs to understand in order to build their portfolio?

Angel investing as an "asset class" exists in a market along with many alternatives for putting your money to work. Like every investment, it has a **risk/return profile** that needs to be understood. Angel investing is somewhat unique in that your behavior as an active investor can actually affect company performance. Unlike a Wall Street trader, an angel investor can help the companies in her portfolio with advice and introductions. Nevertheless, the angel asset class has an overall risk/return profile.

This chapter will give you a perspective on the returns side of it. And as you might guess from the observation about getting involved, it also has its own effort/reward profile too - angel investing can be a lot of work, but also the most fun thing you have ever done in a professional context.

> **Angel investing is somewhat unique in that your behavior as an active investor can actually affect company performance. Unlike a Wall Street trader, an angel investor can help the companies in her portfolio with advice and introductions.**

Another unique aspect of angel investing, and a critical concept to understand, is the **theory of follow-on investing**. As we've pointed out in Chapter 2, the first round of investment in a company is generally over-priced in order to make the founder economics work. A big part of why you overpay is you are buying an information advantage that you can leverage to deploy additional capital in the future more intelligently.

As you watch the company put your money to work, you can see if the CEO is a good steward of capital, whether she gets good results, how she communicates, how customers react to the value proposition and all manner of subtle intangibles picked up along the way. If you have other companies and CEOs to compare to, you can quickly develop a sense of which of your companies are likely to be winners. These insights allow you to follow-on with smarter money in later rounds.

Yes, the valuation will have gone up for those later rounds, but your visibility into performance and remaining risk will also have gone way up. And, the company will be much more established, so even though the valuation is higher, your overall risk/return ratio on the money may be far better than from your first check. In fact, even if the cash-on-cash return multiple on that later round is lower, it may still have a higher IRR.

The final foundational concept is the concept of **angel portfolio diversification**. Just like in mainstream investments in the traditional liquid part of your portfolio, diversification with angel investing is key to your returns. There are two key differences with angel investing, however:

- With angel investing, diversification has many different dimensions besides just quantity of different holdings.

- Given how much labor is involved with the different aspects of these deals and company pathways, it is much, much harder to get diversified into quality deals as an angel investor.

Q

Okay, that's a nice summary. I'd like to dig a bit deeper into each of these concepts. What are some key takeaways that investors should think about in the case of Risk vs. Return?

As a very smart investor we work with, Bob Gervis, has correctly observed, investing is about evaluating return and risk together, in context. As a general matter, asset classes may differ, but your investment processes should stay the same. In every asset class you are looking to understand the overall risks and expected returns for the class, so you can recognize opportunities with the potential to deliver excess returns for the risks presented.

Different investors will vary in how they tackle this challenge. Many angel investors take the view that it is very hard at the earliest stages to really assess risks and as a result feel they must adopt a "low conviction, low concentration" approach. In other words, they hedge risk by making a large number of relatively low conviction bets and avoid having any one investment represent a big concentration of their portfolio. At its most extreme, this approach is sometimes referred to derisively as a "spray and pray" approach, but it should not be dismissed out of hand. Sometimes this approach pays quite well because it increases the chances of hitting one big winner, and in angel investing, one big winner can dwarf the impact of all your small winners put together.

Other investors, particularly ones with a lot of experience who are getting more confident trusting their gut, prefer a much more analytical approach with more conviction in each investment and a portfolio with fewer, more concentrated investments. The investment approach Ham and I use tends to fall toward this end of the spectrum. To do this kind of approach well unfortunately requires a lot of thought and a lot of diligence. To determine if you are looking at a potentially investable opportunity you have to start by considering traditional factors like: the management team, the market, quality of solution, whether there is any kind of moat to hold competitors at bay, and what the exit potential might be.

Then you need to gauge the types and magnitudes of risks presented. Experienced investors will tell you they tend to prefer "execution" type risks in fixable areas like go-to-market strategy, choice of vertical, or marketing strategy rather than more fundamental risks such as technical or science risks.

> To understand the likely returns, you need to analyze the capital structure, future capital requirements, exit potential, and other factors in order to determine the current valuation necessary to deliver minimum required return to compensate for risks presented.

Once you understand what you are signing up for, you need to put it in context. What is an appropriate return for the risks presented? Generally with zero liquidity, long term, high risk investments like angel deals will be much higher than the typical returns you could get in a fully liquid investment class like blue chip stocks or mutual funds. To understand the likely returns, you need to analyze the capital structure, future capital requirements, exit potential, and other factors in order to determine the current valuation necessary to deliver minimum required return to compensate for risks presented (or, the size of exit required to provide an adequate return at the indicated valuation).

And finally if the expected risk-adjusted return ratio looks attractive, then two final tests are necessary:

- **Deal particulars** - are there any things about the deal that are off? Is the board solid? Is there good governance? Are there any red flags in the investing syndicate?

- **Follow-on options** - will this deal allow you to "stage" capital by making additional, much larger, much smarter bets over time? If not, is it worth the trouble and risk to make just this one investment?

Q

When you are making a decision on investing in a company, are there financial risks that you aren't willing to take, and why?

As you may have gleaned from reading our discussion about valuing companies in Chapter 2, it typically does not make a ton of sense for angels to invest in deals which are truly overpriced or which have massive financing risk down the road.

If a deal is over-priced, or priced for perfect execution (as I like to say, has no room for error in the plan), your return is not only going to suffer in a win, but your risk of failure actually ***goes up***. Companies fail all the time because they get way ahead on their post-money valuation and they cannot raise new money on attractive terms and things suddenly curdle and fall apart.

That slight adjustment ***down*** in returns and ***up*** in risk has a MASSIVE impact on the risk/return ratio. It does not make sense to invest in these deals. You might get out alive with a mediocre return, but you will not be paid adequately for the risks and illiquidity you undertook in the process (let alone the work and anxiety!) This recognition is part of the reason why you see year to year variability in the rate at which angel groups like Launchpad Venture Group add new deals to our portfolio. In times when deals are relatively over-priced (such as 2000-2001 or the 2015-2017 period), we tend to concentrate more on follow-on investing into companies who can really support their valuation than on aggressively adding new deals that may prove to be totally over-priced.

Similarly, another financial risk we are are careful about is capital intensity. Companies which are clearly going to need tons and tons of additional financing are dangerous ground for angels unless the source of financing is already identified. Too much can go wrong. Companies like Uber and Tesla that gobble up tons of cash certainly can work out and pay off pretty handsomely, but more often they don't. It does not take a very big hiccup in results or shift in the macro-economic climate to make deals like that which need access to a steady stream of big capital at attractive prices come tumbling down like a house of cards. That game is best left to VCs and private equity teams with billions of dry powder under management.

Q

Now, I'd like to take a closer look at Portfolio Diversification. What are some of the important dimensions that angel investors should consider when building a diverse portfolio?

There are many different elements to diversification beyond just simple quantity of companies. Here are some of the big ones:

- Having companies in different industries or sectors

- Having companies at different stages of development - some which will "pop" early and some which will take a longer path

- Having companies led by different types of entrepreneurs

- Having companies which are undertaking different kinds of key risks

- Having some companies which allow you to be very involved and leverage your expertise, and having some where you can afford to be more passive.

As you are putting together your portfolio, you are trying to make sure you are broad enough to have balance. For every weight, you want a counter-weight. For example, you want to be in several different industries, so that if one industry starts to slow down, others can help pick up the slack. Similarly, you are looking to have some very early stage companies on longer timelines as well as some later stage companies which can be expected to exit sooner and return capital to the portfolio in the near term.

Investing in different types of entrepreneurs is also important. You don't want all late career entrepreneurs any more than you want all millennials as company CEO. You don't want all men or all women. You don't want all engineers or all marketing types. You don't want people who are all from the same social, educational or cultural background. You want to make sure you are investing in a mix of people and that each one (or each total team) has appropriate skills for the opportunity at hand.

> **It is far better to invest in a mix of active and passive deals. A good way to think about it is to look realistically at your schedule and when you are at your maximum capacity, do not take on another "project" deal until one has exited or at least moved out of the diapers stage!**

We've discussed the type of risk being undertaken often enough to not want to repeat it here as a diversification factor beyond acknowledging that type of risk is one important dimension of diversification. Instead, I will focus on a final, more subtle, issue, the issue of *effort*. Different angel investments will require different amounts of your time and effort. Some deals are clearly "projects" but you take them on because you have specific expertise that can really help. Other deals will have someone else who is a better suited person in the lead position and therefore require minimal input and supervision from you. The deals requiring lots of involvement can be lots of fun, but you obviously cannot build a large portfolio full of high-effort deals. You will burn yourself out long before you reap any financial returns. It is far better to invest in a mix of active and passive deals. A good way to think about it is to look realistically at your schedule and when you are at your maximum capacity, do not take on another "project" deal until one has exited or at least moved out of the diapers stage!

Q

Let's say you have ten companies in your portfolio. Ultimately, do you end up investing the exact same amount of money in each company?

No. Even if you start out with the exact same first check size, if you are applying good follow-on theory, you will end up with less money in some and quite a bit more in others. As I noted above, with your first investment, you are buying an informational advantage. You have a front row seat to see how the company does. As the losers become obvious, you should fight the urge to throw good money after bad. As the winners become apparent, you begin following on with smarter money as your conviction builds, leading to a higher portfolio concentration for those winning investments (even on just a cost basis before accounting for the fact that their growing value further increases their share of the portfolio pie). One good way to gauge how you are doing on this is to look at the average amount of money invested in all your losers and the average amount of money invested in your winners. Hopefully, you should see a ratio of at least 2:1 more money into winners, but if you have serious capital to invest, it could reach 5:1 or even 10:1.

That kind of aggressive following-on in winners is sometimes referred to as playing offense. When you see a winner you try to at least maintain if not increase your percentage ownership. Of course there are situations where you need to play defense as well. Sometimes a company gets into a jam and, even though they are not setting the world on fire, you choose to invest a bit more. Why might you put money into a company which is not doing all that well? Because doing so allows you at least a chance of salvaging some or all of your investment in the company. There are situations where investor abandonment would mean a sure and certain write-off of everything invested. If investors put a bit more in they may enable the company to finish a product, or gain enough sales traction to be sold, or do an orderly dismantling that brings in enough to cover the investor preference stack. One other reason you might put money into a struggling company is because some deals present "pay to play" situations where new rescue money says they will only come in if all investors invest their pro-rata, or include provisions which aggressively and disproportionately dilute investors who do not follow-on.

Defensive situations can be especially tough because making a rational decision requires first admitting the original investment was a mistake, and then taking a sober and clear-eyed approach to your defense strategy. Each case is different and should be evaluated carefully. Although there are situations where defensive investing makes good sense, more often than not, it is probably smarter to admit your failings and take the write-off. It is a different kind of mindset and a different kind of analysis. Often people making defensive investments either don't realize that is what they are doing (because they still hope the company will get back on track and it is all going to work out) or they don't realize it is a lost cause and that losing $25K now is better than losing $50K in two years.

So those are the decision factors for clearly offensive and clearly defensive situations. If only it were so easy. One of the persistent difficulties with following on is that many times it is not clear whether you are playing offense or defense. Frequently, it is not easy to determine if you are looking at a winner or a loser by the time a company needs more money. Forgive the gambling analogy, but if you have ever played Texas Hold'em, you will understand the concept of paying ante just to see the next card. In angel investing often you need to decide whether to put more money in before you can be reasonably sure, let alone absolutely certain, that the company is a winner.

In those situations, the best course of action is to have a long term capital staging plan for the company and add an incremental amount of additional capital toward your target amount. Your initial check might represent 10% or maybe 25% of your end goal for money into the company and in these situations you put another similar or even smaller amount in. You are hedging your bet - it is not yet time to significantly ratchet up your commitment, but it is also clearly too early to write things off. So you often just bite the bullet and invest.

But before you do write that second check, you should review the company's stewardship of the first capital it was entrusted with. Did the company perform as well as could be expected given the circumstances which developed? Were there any red flags about the team, the market, the competition? If there were, perhaps this is a case where you choose to allocate that money to a new company instead. But if there are not any red flags, then put in another small sized check reflecting medium conviction rather than bumping up the check size yet. Or in Texas Hold 'em parlance, ante up, but don't raise.

Chapter 5

Tent Poles and Toads: The Mix of a Winning Startup Portfolio

How do you define success as an angel investor? Are you successful if you invested in one grand slam like Amazon or Google? Perhaps you define success as not losing all of your angel investment dollars after making investments in a dozen companies. Or, maybe success for you is defined by how many entrepreneurs you helped get companies financed and on their way. Since angel investors have many different criteria for defining success, it's difficult to compare one investor's results to another's.

With all that said, I'd like to propose we narrow the focus temporarily and take a purely mathematical approach to defining success. This approach is similar to the method used to measure the performance of traditional VC funds. There's a significant amount of data collected over the years for VC performance from organizations such as Cambridge Associates and Thomson Reuters Venture Economics. And, even though there is limited data on angel investing returns, we do have some preliminary research that indicates average returns for angel investors are around 27% for an annual rate of return.

If you are motivated by financial performance in angel investing, just as Ham and I are, what level of investment returns do you need to achieve before you declare success? Let's ask Ham what financial yardstick he likes to measure his performance against and find out how he expects his investment returns to materialize over the years.

Q

Ham, what data from the VC world do you think will help angel investors understand what performance metrics they should use as guidelines when measuring their own performance?

Let me start by briefly explaining how VC funds are structured. A typical fund has a fixed amount of capital (e.g. $250M) to invest. Most funds have a 10 year life span where most of the new investments are made in the first three years and follow-on investments are made in the subsequent years, with increasing focus on enabling exits as the fund reaches maturity. The expectation of the VC is that most, if not all, of their investments will have an exit before the end of the 10 year fund life. Though, it should come as no surprise to know that many funds are extended by an additional 2-3 years before being shut down.

Because the risks investing in startup companies are much greater than the risks of investing in public companies, and the money is totally tied up and illiquid throughout, VC funds need to outperform the public stock market indices (S&P 500, NASDAQ 100, etc.) by a significant amount to make economic sense. So an annual 10% rate of return for an investor in a VC fund is not enough. They are looking for annual return percentages in the high teens or low twenties. And keep in mind that their performance threshold is raised by the fact that they are taking management fees out as they go along, and also taking a carry out of profits, which further reduces the take-home performance of their LPs.

Based on detailed research from Cambridge Associates, the top quartile of VC funds have an average annual return ranging from 15% to 27% over the past 10 years. So, if you are an investor in one of these top quartile funds, your returns are better than what you would expect to achieve in the public market indices. However, if you invested in one of the bottom quartile VC funds over the past 10 years, your returns are mostly in the low single digits. You would have been better off in a fund that tracks the S&P 500 (and you would have paid a lot less in fees)!

> **Based on detailed research from Cambridge Associates, the top quartile of VC funds have an average annual return ranging from 15% to 27% over the past 10 years.**

In addition to analyzing annual rates of return, it's helpful with VC funds to look at the Distributed to Paid-In (DPI) ratio and the Total Value to Paid-In (TVPI) ratio. The DPI ratio is a calculation of the total amount of capital returned to the investors divided by the amount of capital invested into the fund. The TVPI ratio includes capital returned to the investors along with any remaining value still in the fund. As you can see in the Cambridge Associates chart on the next page, the TVPI ratio (light blue bars), goes as high as 4.5x in the boom years of the Internet bubble and down to 1.5x during the post bubble years. It should be noted, if you want to be a top decile fund, your final DPI ratio needs to be around 3x. In

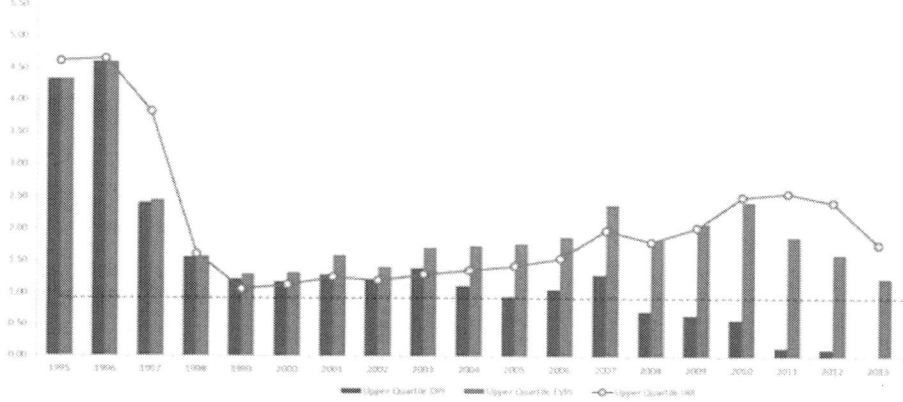

Upper Quartile Fund Performance 1995-2015

other words, for every 1 dollar invested in a VC fund, there needs to be a return of 3 dollars over the subsequent 10 year time period. Taken together these VC performance indices should give angels a sense of what the professional money managers achieve when working with these startup companies (albeit at a slightly later stage.)

Q

The data from Cambridge Associates talks about the overall returns from venture funds. How should angel investors think about the returns they will get from an individual company in their portfolio?

So what you should expect the exits to look like in a portfolio of 10 companies? In summary, if you are using a good process and working out of a strong deal flow, you can expect to end up with approximately 5 strikeouts, 4 base hits and 1 home run in any batch of ten companies. For a more detailed analysis, Correlation Ventures researched more than 21,000 exits of VC-backed companies between 2004 and 2013.

Based on the data from Correlation Ventures, you can see in the chart below that approximately 65% of companies return 0 to 1 times the capital invested. Those are your strikeouts. Another 25% of companies return 1 to 5 times the capital invested. Those are your base hits. The remaining 10% return more than 5 times the capital invested. And, that's where your home runs come from. If you are really lucky, over the course of a few 10 company "baskets" you have one of the 50x+ returns that qualify as a grand slam.

It's important to note that these results are for VC-backed companies. Angel investors fund a wider range of companies, and in many cases, invest at earlier stages, with lower valuations and higher alpha, than VCs with correspondingly higher valuations at their initial time of investment. Based on the data that we have collected at Seraf over the years, we see a somewhat lower percentage of failures in our dataset and a slightly larger number of home runs versus what Correlation

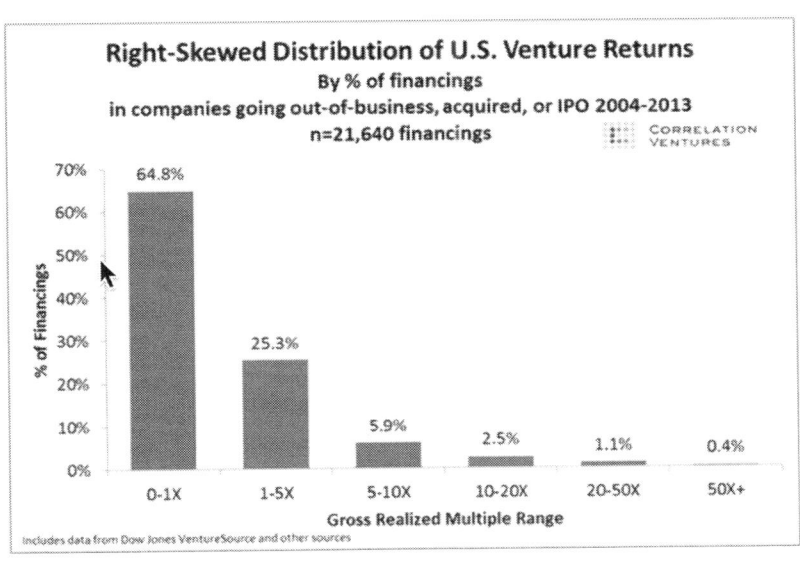

Ventures reports for the VC industry. Though, in fairness, the Seraf portfolio management platform may cater to the more organized, serious and professional half of the angel market.

Q

Now we know what a great VC fund looks like (it should return 3x capital invested). And, we know what the return distribution should look like for early stage investments (a mix of strikeouts, base hits and home runs.) How do we combine that information to help an angel investor construct a great performing portfolio?

My job explaining how to build an angel portfolio would be so much easier if angels invested through a fund model similar to what VCs do. So, to help grasp the math behind structuring a successful fund, I am going to make the following assumptions for this simplified example angel investor portfolio.

- The angel will invest in 10 companies, which we believe is really the minimum needed for baseline diversification.
- Most likely all of the initial investments will be made over a 2 to 3 year time period.
- To keep it simple, each company will receive the same amount of investment. So for a small angel portfolio of $250K, each company will receive a $25K investment.
- There won't be any follow-on rounds of investment and the entire portfolio of companies will exit within 10 years of the first investment made by the angel.

Given those assumptions, how can this angel end up making 3 times her money in ten years? What does the math have to look like to achieve this level of success? Without the aid of smart follow-on investments, it is not easy. Using the expected distribution of exits that we see from the Correlation Ventures chart above, we come up with the following for a top quintile (3X DPI) angel portfolio.

- 5 companies in the portfolio are total losses and return $0 to the investor. However, you are able to get 20% of your investment back through an offset vs. any capital gains you have. This means each company will return $5K in tax write-offs for a total of $25K.

- You might not like the fact that I used tax benefits as part of the investment returns. So instead, consider that at least one or two of these failed companies will return some capital. That's another way you can get $25K back from your initial $125K investment in these 5 companies and still consider the investments in the strikeout category.

- 3 of the remaining 5 companies average out to 3X on invested capital, so each company returns on average $75K for a total of $225K. Combined with the 25K from the losers you are now at a break-even $250K or 1X.

- 1 company produces a 5X return, not a bad exit, but nothing to set the world on fire. This company returns $125K.

- 1 company is the real winner in the portfolio (15X) and does the heavy lifting you need to achieve a high rate of return. Without this exit, it's hard to justify the risk that an angel investor takes with their capital. This company returns $375K.

- So the combined return on all 10 companies is $750K. That's a 3X return on the angel investor's original investment of $250K.

Many angel investors believe they have to invest in the next billion dollar company to achieve big returns on their angel investments. The reality, based on the assumptions outlined above, is that you don't. In my personal portfolio, I've had two home run exits (i.e. 10-20X level). One company was acquired for less than $50M and the other for less than $200M. Find two companies like that in a 10 company portfolio and you are well on your way to awesome angel investment returns!

In the example outlined above, if the investor had more money for greater diversification or some follow-on investment in some of the winners, there would be a bit more room for error. But still, this simple angel portfolio example should help you understand how fund math works. For a more detailed approach to modeling a portfolio, we've put together a sample spreadsheet described in the Appendix that will allow you to model a variety of scenarios. Check it out and see what other ways you can achieve a successful financial outcome for your angel investments.

Chapter 6

Pure Upside: Understanding Stock Options and Restricted Stock

The first time you receive stock options as an employee is a magical moment. You feel suddenly part of something bigger than just earning a paycheck. You daydream about how various financial scenarios might play out. You take a sudden interest in the wellbeing of your company and the factors which affect its stock price.

Early in my career I worked with, wrote, and interpreted many stock option programs and thought I understood them very well. Intellectually I did, but that did nothing to prepare me emotionally for being on the receiving end of my first grant of options as I transitioned to becoming a young tech company employee. The sensation of recognition, reward, even worth, has a powerful impact on a young professional.

It is no surprise therefore that startups are nearly universal in their adoption of stock options as a tool for attracting, motivating and retaining new hires. And with all these start up stock option pools everywhere, it is natural for an angel to wonder if they are a relevant part of an angel's overall investing strategy.

The short answer is yes, in two important ways. First, in connection with setting the valuation of a company, and second as a direct recipient of stock options (or their cousins the restricted stock grant or stock warrant). We have talked quite a bit elsewhere about the impact of option pools on valuation, so here I want to focus on the direct use of these derivative securities on the strategies and returns of angel investors. Let's see if we can tackle a few of the key questions about options and restricted stock for angels.

> **Startups are nearly universal in their adoption of stock options as a tool for attracting, motivating and retaining new hires. And with all these start up stock option pools everywhere, it is natural for an angel to wonder if they are a relevant part of an angel's overall investing strategy.**

Q

Christopher, occasionally, angel investors end up taking board seats or becoming advisors in companies when they make an investment. Should they expect to be paid? What is the rationale for paying them?

There is a long-standing tradition by established companies of paying the independent directors for their board service with equity, typically options or restricted stock. It is viewed as essential for attracting the best talent and compensating them for their time and value-add. And it is believed that using stock that vests over time is a good way to align directors with shareholder interests. If the directors want their compensation to be worth anything, they will focus on mid-to-long term share price appreciation.

With less established startup companies, some of this tradition applies, but with some important caveats. In an established company, much of the board will consist of independent directors who are compensated by the company using some combination of stock and cash. With a startup, the board typically consists of roughly equal parts management and investors, with maybe one independent director mixed in.

Q

How does this affect compensation?

For the management and independent directors, compensation practice is roughly the same: salary, bonus and stock for management and some stock for the independent director. However, the investor component of the board is a bit different for a few reasons:

- First, they appointed themselves by contractual right,

- Second, they are already major shareholders, and

- Third, in the case of VCs, they are already being paid a management fee, and some carry for things like board service. It is their day job.

Q

What difference do those three factors make in compensation?

It tends to weaken the argument that generous compensation is required. For VCs it is hard to force yourself onto a board and then demand that you be compensated with stock. Especially when you are already a major shareholder and your LPs are paying you to do the board work.

However, board compensation tends to be a little more generous for angels investors relative to VCs in recognition of several key differences between angels and VCs:

- The angel is representing and doing the work on behalf of many individual investors;
- The angel is volunteering her time and not being paid a management fee or carry by any LPs;
- The angel is likely a much smaller shareholder for whom a few options would make a real economic difference; and
- The angel is typically helping the company with valuable skills, connections and expertise at a very early stage when help from the board is sorely needed.

> **Payment is almost invariably in the form of equity rather than cash. Paying directors cash would be a terrible use of that scarce resource early on, and also a lost opportunity for alignment with shareholders.**

Q

How much, and in what form, will this compensation be paid out to the director or advisor?

Payment is almost invariably in the form of equity rather than cash. Paying directors cash would be a terrible use of that scarce resource early on, and also a lost opportunity for alignment with shareholders. The form of equity paid is usually either stock options vesting over time, or increasingly, restricted stock where the restrictions lapse over time. The typical approach is to give an initial grant at the time of joining the board, and then do supplementary grants annually or once every couple of years.

In our experience, early-stage directors are typically given an initial grant in an amount equal to somewhere between 0.25% and 1.0% of the company's total shares outstanding on a fully diluted basis. Board chairs or extremely active directors with specific industry contacts and introductions may be at the higher end of the prevailing range. Executive directors and special advisors are special cases and may fall outside of the range. It is the responsibility of the board to ensure the appropriateness of all compensation paid by the company. Assuming a grant is appropriate, it may have a very big impact; for an angel investing their own money in order to buy a likely similar or lower percentage of the company, a grant like that can be a huge multiplier on your returns - doubling or even tripling a good outcome.

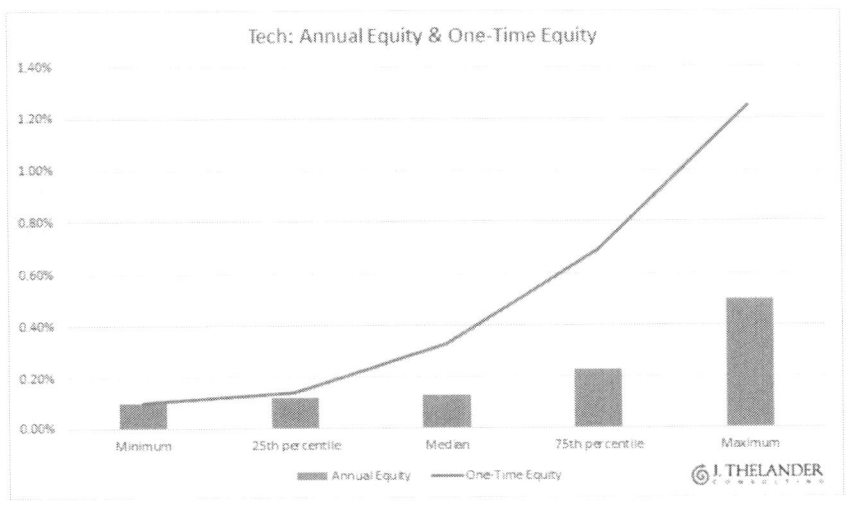

Subsequent supplementary grants would be at the lowest end of that spectrum. Based on market studies, our experience of how angel directors are paid would appear to be fairly consistent with prevailing market norms for non-investor directors; Pitchbook has done a study and come up with pretty similar findings (see chart on previous page.)

For more detail on the other considerations to keep in mind when designing or dealing with director compensation, we've done a thorough overview of the issues and pitfalls.

Q

So options and restricted stock have big potential for angels sitting on boards. Are there tax issues a board member should take into consideration with the stock compensation they will receive for their service to the company?

In a word, YES!

The key threshold issue is to consider the form of equity security. Stock options and restricted stock are economically quite similar, but have very different mechanics and therefore very different tax considerations. Restricted stock is increasingly used instead of options because of its greater tax efficiency.

With options, you are being granted a right to buy a certain amount of stock for a certain price at certain time(s) in the future. You do not own the stock until vesting occurs and you exercise the stock option. You pay nothing up front, but you do not own any stock either.

Restricted shares are granted up front, but subject to restrictions which fall away over time. In other words, options have ownership rights which vest over time, and restricted shares have ownership restrictions which lapse over time.

Q

What is the key difference between stock options and restricted stock?

They are really very similar in their ultimate effect; the key difference is the tax efficiency. Restricted shares allow the recipient of the shares to recognize and declare the imputed income from the transfer of restricted shares on day one. That allows the director to make an election under IRS Section 83(b) and pay a small amount of income taxes up front (reflecting the current fair market value of stock that is subject to restrictions). And, under the 83(b) rules, pay the lower capital gains rate on any future profits, including potentially the lower long term rates for stock held for the requisite period. For more on working with Section 83(b) see the Appendix.

> **Suffice it to say, restricted stock is a lot less work - a one time tax payment up front rather than a tax payment each time options are exercised. And, because restricted stock allows you to get that capital gains clock running, it may also allow you to leverage lower tax rates.**

With these non-qualified stock options, all the ownership timing is compressed. To take advantage of capital gains treatment, you must:

- Wait for the stock to vest,
- Then pay the exercise price,
- Then pay tax on any income that is imputed from the difference between your exercise price and the fair market value at the time
- And then begin your holding period for capital gains treatment.

Suffice it to say, restricted stock is a lot less work - a one time tax payment up front rather than a tax payment each time options are exercised. And, because restricted stock allows you to get that capital gains clock running, it may also allow you to leverage lower tax rates.

Because non-qualified options are so much more work, most option grantees just end up holding onto options and doing a cashless exercise at the last minute (e.g. at the time of company exit or on the eve of option expiration - typically ten years). They use some of the profits to satisfy the exercise price and just dispose of the whole bundle of options at once. Of course that means they are going to pay ordinary income tax rates on the whole transaction.

Q

So if you don't get restricted stock, you end up with Non-Qualified stock options. What are some important considerations when exercising your stock options?

With options, once they vest, you must first decide whether you are even going to exercise the option before the time when you are ultimately forced to (by exit or expiration). Then you must decide if you are going to sell the shares immediately or hold on to the shares you just exercised.

If you exercise and sell them immediately (assuming that is permitted under the terms of your investment and there is a market for the shares - remember we are talking about private companies here) then you will pay:

* The exercise price and
* Taxes at ordinary tax rates on the difference between your exercise price and the Fair Market Value (FMV) at the time of exercise.

This is true for both qualified employee shares and the non-qualified shares a board director would get.

If you exercise and sell the shares immediately, all the income is deemed compensation (ordinary income) for both types of awards. So for example:

- If you have 10,000 options at an exercise price of a $1 and the FMV is now $5,

- If you exercise the options you will pay $10,000 to the company to exercise them and pay taxes (at ordinary rates) on $4 of difference per share or $40,000 in profit.

- That could cost you approximately $12,000 of taxes.

- So the take home amount after selling your shares for $50,000, less the cost of $10,000 for the exercise, less $12,000 of taxes, is a figure of $28,000 in net profit.

An option is a pure upside play. Fortunately you don't have to commit to paying the exercise price on your options until you see whether the options are profitable. Initial instinct would dictate holding onto them and deciding as late as possible whether you want to exercise. However that instinct runs into direct conflict with tax considerations.

> An option is a pure upside play. Fortunately you don't have to commit to paying the exercise price on your options until you see whether the options are profitable.

It may seem counter-intuitive, but tax advisors often tell clients to exercise the options as early as you dare. If you can afford the exercise price, and you are willing to take the risk of paying good money for illiquid private company stock that might be worthless, then exercising early allows you to do two important things from a tax efficiency standpoint:

- First, you can exercise when fair market value (FMV) is still low and the per share "spread" or profit is small so the ordinary income tax bill will be small.

- Second, it allows you to get the capital gains tax clock running on those shares so that you can hopefully qualify for long term capital gains before you are forced to sell as part of a company exit scenario.

What does this mean in dollar terms? Let's look at an example:

* Suppose you have options with an exercise price of $1, and the FMV is $5.

* If you think the company is poised to take off or do a financing soon, then you may take the view that FMV is relatively low in the grand scheme of things and want to exercise the options.

* You will pay taxes on the $4 spread. And then you will start holding the stock for capital gains holding period purposes.

* If the company takes off and is acquired for $15 a share, you are going to be very glad that you get to apply the capital gains tax rate to $10 of the total $14 in profit rather than ordinary income tax on all $14.

On the other hand, if the company is struggling a bit and is clearly going to need some time before it qualifies for a real up round, let alone a great exit, you might decide to hold off a bit and not let the "tax tail wag the dog."

If the company is struggling, that means future value increases are still speculative and the risk of failure looms large. In that case, taking hard-earned after-tax money and using it to pay the exercise price to purchase and hold sketchy private company stock, does not make much sense. In this scenario the loss risk is greater than the tax efficiency risk. Better to wait a little while for the situation to come into focus and take your chances that you will still be able to exercise in time for a good FMV spread and a long enough capital gains holding period.

Q

Are there any other issues that stock option holders need to consider?

One other thing to keep in mind at all times is that all the options have an expiration date. Many option plans at companies specify a ten year life, and you don't want to be forced into acting quickly. Never a bad idea when you get options to set a calendar reminder for 15-18 months before the final expiration date so at a minimum you can just punt and exercise at the last minute and still get at least a one year capital gains tax holding period. It is a shame to forget about this issue and lose the benefit of a well-thought out execution strategy. Also, remember the above relates to non-qualified options.

Q

So that covers 83(b) elections on restricted stock and capital gains treatment on option exercises. Are there other issues to be mindful of in a positive outcome situation?

Yes, there is one other major tax issue you want to be aware of, and that is the considerable benefit available under IRS Section 1202. This part of the US tax code introduces not only huge potential savings, but also really long five year holding period requirements which affect your option exercise timing considerably.

> **There is one other major tax issue you want to be aware of, and that is the considerable benefit available under IRS Section 1202.**

Section 1202 deals with a gain on a stock sale. If your investment qualifies for 1202 treatment, up to 100% of the gain could be excluded up to the greater of $10,000,000 or 10 times your investment. To qualify, this stock must

1. Be a domestic C Corporation from inception;

2. The gross assets of the Company must be under $50 million at the time the investment is made; and

3. The stock must be issued for either cash, property, or services.

4. Additionally, the company must be an active operating business (i.e. not an investment business or one similar to a service business such as a law firm.)

5. And finally, you must have held the stock for at least five years. Collectively, these requirements are the QSB or Qualified Small Business test. If your stock meets all these tests, it is QSBS or Qualified Small Business Stock.

Under 1202, the percentage of your gain you are allowed to exclude depends on when you acquired the qualifying stock. As long as you hold your stock for a minimum of 5 years before the sale occurs, your capital gains exclusion is calculated as follows:

- Acquired between 8/10/1993 and 2/17/2009:   50% Exclusion

- Acquired between 2/18/2009 and 9/27/2010:   75% Exclusion

- Acquired after 9/28/2010:   100% Exclusion

But 1202 does have a few catches that many people are not aware of. If you held convertible debt early on in a company and then it converted into stock later on, the period during which you held the note does not count toward your 1202 five year holding requirement that clock starts when you convert to equity (though the note period does count toward your long term cap gain determination). And you need to keep in mind that other measures don't tie back, such as the $50 million in assets test, which is tested at the date of conversion of the debt to stock.

Another thing to know is that if you own 1202 QSB stock, and then decide to gift it to another individual later, the stock will retain its character of 1202 stock to the donee. Thus a parent who owns 1202 stock can gift it to his or her children, and they can benefit from the same reduced capital gains exclusions that the parent would have.

A final point: these 1202 rules are quite complicated, subject to change, and their applicability to your situation may depend on the particular details of your investment, so it is best to get help from professional advisors before making assumptions.

Q

From time to time I receive warrants as a part of an investment. What are they and when is the 'right' time to exercise warrants?

Warrants are basically identical to non-qualified stock options from an economic and tax perspective. The only difference is that warrants are typically one-off instruments and not issued under the terms of the stock option plan (though they may or may not use shares set aside in the option pool.) Options are commonly used as compensation for employees, directors, advisors and consultants, and warrants tend to be used more frequently in business transaction contexts. For example, warrants might be issued to a bank in connection with taking out a line of credit, or might be included in an investment deal as a sweetener to encourage investors to jump into the first close or to help span a gap in valuation expectations. One cosmetic difference between options and warrants is that warrants have all of their terms in the warrant document, whereas option agreements usually rely on having some terms spelled out in the umbrella option plan documentation.

In terms of exercising warrants, the analysis is similar to a non-qualified option. Generally speaking, the best strategy for exercising warrants is to wait until you are sure the company is pretty well out of the woods (and the warrants will therefore likely be worth something) and then, once you have made that determination, exercise them as soon as possible to start the capital gains clock running. By doing the exercise early you are hoping to get at least a year of ownership before any acquisition occurs. That way they are treated as long term capital gains with a preferential rate, as opposed to short term capital gains, which are taxed at the same rate as ordinary income. Put another way, you want to exercise them as soon as you reach the point that you are sure you are going to exercise them.

So why not just exercise them right away? Because you have to spend money to exercise them. If the exercise price is fair market value (FMV) at the time they are granted, that can still be real money - equivalent to simply investing in the company at that price. If the warrants are issued way below FMV, say for a penny each, then you might as well exercise them right away.

Q

My final question for you relates to taxes. What do you think the most important tax issue is for angel investors in the US?

There are really three key tax provisions for angels; two provisions relate to gains on winning investments (Section 1202 and Section 1045) and one relates to losses on losing investments (Section 1244).

We've discussed 1202 above - it is a massive benefit allowing you to exclude up to 100% of your gains if you can hit the requirements, especially the type of company and the five year holding period

(possibly less than 100% depending on the year - see above).

Currently, this 1202 tax benefit has been labeled by Congress as "permanent" but when it comes to tax policy and government tax revenue trade-offs, nothing is a given. Get advice before banking on using 1202.

Continuing on the topic of treatment of gains from your wins, let's look at Section 1045. Although it relates to gains, this provision works like a "rollover" provision for your gains. Many will be familiar with the fact that you can reduce the amount of taxes on your capital gain from selling your primary residence as long as you purchase a new home within a certain number of months of the sale of your original home. 1045 is a similar "rollover" provision for QSBS investments.

The 1045 provision allows you to avoid paying any capital gains as long as you put all of your gains into a new QSBS investment within 60 days. Furthermore, the holding period of the replacement stock includes the holding period of the stock you just sold. This is a great way to help you get the preferential tax treatment of Section 1202 for your long term capital gains. But be careful... 60 days is a ridiculously short period of time even for full-time angels with huge deal flow, so it is going to take some lucky timing to be able to use 1045 - you shouldn't jump into an impulsive new investment just to save on your taxes. That's a great way to turn those gains into a big loss!

Q

Okay... so I have one more question! Speaking of losses, what are the relevant tax provisions for angel losses? And are they any good?

Section 1244 is the big one, and it is excellent. Admittedly, it is never fun to write off one of your investments, but it happens about half the time in a portfolio of early stage investments. Luckily there is some salvage value to be had.

> **Section 1244 allows you to write off your angel losses in qualifying companies against the higher ordinary earned income and its associated higher tax rate.**

In this worst case scenario, of course, anyone can always write off their losses vs. any capital gains they receive in the same calendar year: net losses and net gains are always an off-set.

But for angels, Section 1244 kicks it up to a whole other level. Section 1244 allows you to write off your angel losses in qualifying companies against the higher ordinary earned income and its associated higher tax rate. That can make a big difference since capital gains are taxed around 20% and earned income rates can be as high as 39.6%.

In order to take advantage of Section 1244, your investment must be part of the first $1M invested into a QSBS company. It's important to document and track the fact that you qualify as early as you can.

Even an email from the CEO or part time CFO is better than nothing. And Seraf helps you with the tracking of your 1244 status by: 1) asking whenever you record a new investment whether it's 1244 qualified and 2) allowing you to store any documents you might have to prove that your investment was 1244 qualified in case your tax returns are audited.

The foregoing three sections have all related to stock in Qualified Small Businesses. Many investors wonder about whether there are any special tax considerations to be aware of when they invest in Convertible Notes. Well, it should come as no surprise that yes, there are. With convertible notes are three areas you need to be aware of.

First, you may have to recognize, and pay tax on, interest payments accruing on your note. And that includes silent background interest accruing without a dime being paid to you. Even though you didn't receive any cash payments from the company, you did get the economic benefit of the accrual, and in the view of the IRS, that is income and it is likely taxable.

Second, in most cases, no capital gain is recognized when the note is converted to stock, but the conversion of the note does typically trigger interest income recognition and taxes on that interest. Note that this applies even if the interest is paid in stock vs. cash - you may have a cash tax obligation even though you received illiquid stock as your form of interest.

Third, be careful when any warrants are issued along with a convertible note, particularly if some investors did not get the warrants (for example because they were not in the first close). The value assigned to the warrants has the effect of creating what is viewed by the IRS as discount on the note. Their logic is as follows: since the warrants have to have some economic value, and you are paying the same as other note holders not getting warrants, you must be getting the note below fair market value. The delta between FMV and the price you paid is considered imputed income, and will be viewed as taxable income. In other words, the warrant sweetener can make the note transaction a taxable event. Ouch!

That is a lot of information. Two provisions for wins, a provision for losses, and some tricky considerations for convertible notes. What's the take-away? Make sure you have an accountant who understands the complexities of QSBS investments. You definitely want to make sure you don't get tripped up by an IRS audit!

Appendix

At Launchpad Venture Group, we provide our members with a series of guides and templates to help improve their performance as investors. In this appendix, we include example guides and templates that we use on a regular basis.

I. **Capitalization Table with Waterfall Analysis**: This is a collection of two spreadsheets that help you model a company's capitalization table and the resulting waterfall analysis based on a variety of exit scenarios for the company. (http://bit.ly/Series_A_Cap_Table_and_Waterfall or http://bit.ly/Series_A_and_B_Cap_Table_and_Waterfall)

II. **Modeling Tool for an Early Stage Investment Portfolio**: This spreadsheet allows you to model potential outcomes for the overall return from an early stage investment portfolio. (http://bit.ly/Seraf_Portfolio_Modeling_Tool)

III. **Sample IRS Section 83(b) Election Form**: An IRS Section 83(b) Election is an approach to minimizing the amount of tax a director will pay as she vests any restricted stock she received as compensation for board service. We provide a standard form and the necessary instructions so you can successfully file your election with the IRS. (http://bit.ly/IRS_83b_Election_Form)

Please note that in addition to including these guides, we also provide an online version. If you click on the URL listed next to each item, you will be able to access an online document that can save you time in creating your own version.

I. Capitalization Tables with Waterfall Analysis

Have you ever been in a situation where you are negotiating an investment with an entrepreneur and you can't agree on the pre-money valuation? Any early stage investor who makes more than one or two investments will certainly run into this issue. It's never an easy discussion, so it helps if you are prepared ahead of time with concrete facts and figures for your recommended valuation. If you do a little homework, not only might you be surprised how little difference small changes in valuation make for founders, you will also be armed to have a very educational discussion with the entrepreneurs.

Let's play out a scenario that Christopher and I ran into recently with a company in which we were looking to invest. At a high level, here are the key facts about the company today, along with a few assumptions we will make about the future of the company.

- The company is pre-revenue and needs to raise $1.25M to get their product shipping and close their first few customer deals.

- We were willing to invest at a $3.6M pre-money valuation. The entrepreneur insisted on a $4M valuation.

- We assumed the company will need an additional $5M Series B financing to get all the way to an exit.

- We assumed the Series B round will be priced at 2X the post-money valuation of the Series A round, and both rounds will be Non-Participating Preferred.

- We assumed that approximately 5% of the common shares are held by employees, directors and advisors.

- We assumed an exit for the company will be somewhere in the $25M to $100M range.

So, given those facts and assumptions, what difference does our requested valuation ($3.6M) versus the entrepreneur's desired valuation ($4M) actually make to the returns of each party?

	$3.6M Series A Valuation	$4M Series A Valuation
$25M Exit		
Founders	$9.3M	$9.9M
Series A Shareholders	$4.6M	$4.3M
$50M Exit		
Founders	$18.7M	$19.7M
Series A Shareholders	$9.1M	$8.7M
$100M Exit		
Founders	$37.3M	$39.5M
Series A Shareholders	$18.2M	$17.3M

Note that our $3.6M pre-money offer is 10% less than the founder's $4M pre-money expectation. The final outcome for the entrepreneur in all of the above exit scenarios shows about a 5% to 6% difference in what they will ultimately receive upon an exit. Even though it feels to the entrepreneur that our respective valuations are miles apart, the reality is about half the difference in the end.

It is probably worth pointing out to the entrepreneur that there are two further advantages for them in keeping the pre-money reasonable:

It makes it easier to bring investors into the round so that they can finish the fund-raising quickly and get back to focusing on the operations of the company. And, it means the post-money valuation will be more reasonable, which means it will be less of a yoke around their necks (see Chapter 2) as they head into the uncertainties that lie ahead and try to grow into justifying their valuation for the next round.

So hopefully you are convinced it is worth doing some modeling. But how can you easily do this type of financial modeling to help better understand valuation and exit scenarios? You need a good Cap Table and Waterfall Analysis tool.

If you perform a Google search for the term "Cap Table", you will end up with dozens of options to choose from. These options include everything from Excel spreadsheets that build simple cap tables all the way along the spectrum to complex, high-end software products that will track everything you need for a complete cap table. But we built one we think you might prefer using.

So why did we bother creating another cap table tool when there are so many options out there? We did it for several reasons:

1. We wanted a tool that was very simple to set up. We didn't want to have to enter lots of data to model a cap table.

2. We wanted a tool that allowed us to model a variety of different exit scenarios to help understand how much each shareholder would get depending on the size of the exit.

3. We wanted a tool that was free for everyone to use with no strings attached.

We chose the familiar Google Sheets platform and created two separate documents. The first sheet allows you to create a cap table with just a single Series A round of financing for very basic modeling.

Valuations, Investments and Share Price

	Series A
Pre-Money Valuation	$3,175,000
Total Invested in Round	$1,250,000
Post-Money Valuation	$4,425,000
Price / Share	$1.25
Liquidation Preference	1
Participating Preferred	Yes

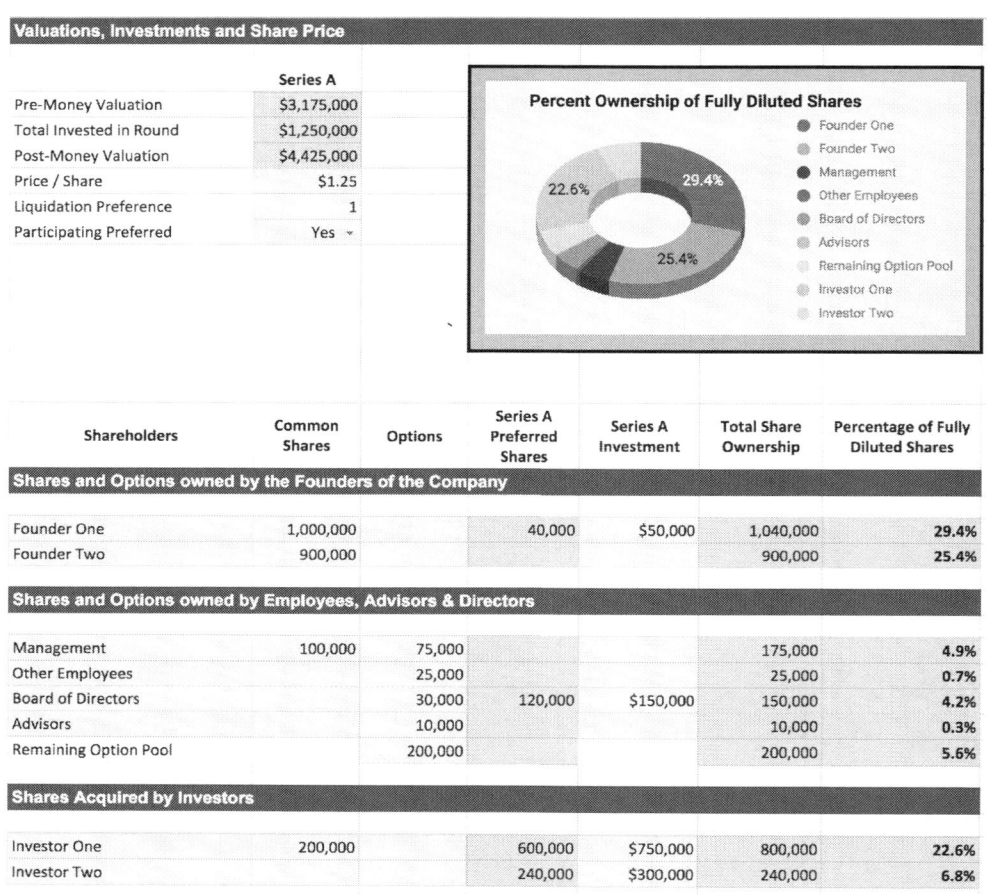

Shareholders	Common Shares	Options	Series A Preferred Shares	Series A Investment	Total Share Ownership	Percentage of Fully Diluted Shares
Shares and Options owned by the Founders of the Company						
Founder One	1,000,000		40,000	$50,000	1,040,000	29.4%
Founder Two	900,000				900,000	25.4%
Shares and Options owned by Employees, Advisors & Directors						
Management	100,000	75,000			175,000	4.9%
Other Employees		25,000			25,000	0.7%
Board of Directors		30,000	120,000	$150,000	150,000	4.2%
Advisors		10,000			10,000	0.3%
Remaining Option Pool		200,000			200,000	5.6%
Shares Acquired by Investors						
Investor One	200,000		600,000	$750,000	800,000	22.6%
Investor Two			240,000	$300,000	240,000	6.8%

Cap Table with a Series A Round of Financing

The second sheet allows you to create a cap table with both a Series A and Series B round. In both sheets, we provide a waterfall analysis so you can model exactly how much capital is returned to each shareholder and each class of stock under a variety of exit scenarios.

These sheets were designed with a fairly common capitalization structure in mind. The sheets support the following key features:

- Either one or two rounds of Series Preferred Stock
- Participating and Non-Participating Preferred Shares
- Liquidation Preferences
- Options, both Issued and Non-Issued
- Waterfall Analysis to model multiple exit scenarios

Summary Cap Table

Security Type	Outstanding Shares	Price per Share	Liquidation Preference	Percent Ownership
Common Shares	2,200,000			66%
Issued Options	140,000			4%
Series A Preferred Shares - Participating	1,000,000	$1.25	$1,250,000	30%
Total Shares Outstanding	3,340,000			

Exit Proceeds

	Price	Price	Price	Price
Purchase Price for the Company	$2,000,000	$4,175,000	$10,000,000	$20,000,000

Liquidation Preference Calculation

Series A Liquidation Preference	$1,250,000	$1,250,000	$1,250,000	$1,250,000
Remaining Proceeds	$750,000	$2,925,000	$8,750,000	$18,750,000
Proceeds per Common Share	$0.22	$0.88	$2.62	$5.61
Proceeds per Series A Share (as converted)	$0.22	$0.88	$2.62	$5.61
Total Proceeds per Series A Share	$1.47	$2.13	$3.87	$6.86

Returned Capital by Round

Common Shares	$494,012	$1,926,647	$5,763,473	$12,350,299
Options	$31,437	$122,605	$366,766	$785,928
Series A Preferred	$1,474,551	$2,125,749	$3,869,760	$6,863,772
Total Proceeds	$2,000,000	$4,175,000	$10,000,000	$20,000,000
Series A Return Multiple	1.2	1.7	3.1	5.5

Waterfall Analysis with a Series A Round of Financing

It's also important to note that for the sake of simplicity and usability these sheets are NOT designed to support the following items commonly found in cap tables:

- More than two rounds of Series Preferred Stock
- Convertible Notes
- Dividends
- Warrants

So, if you are looking for a complete solution that will help you manage every aspect of your company's cap table, just do a Google search and you will find plenty of great products to purchase. In the meantime, try out these free Google sheets to help you build a well structured cap table along with a waterfall analysis for exit scenario modeling.

II. Portfolio Modeling Tool

One of the biggest challenges faced by early stage investors is to assemble a portfolio of investments that in aggregate return more than 2 times the original amount invested in the total portfolio. In the language of Venture Capital, the goal of a successful early stage investor is to achieve a Distributed to Paid-In (DPI) ratio greater than 2X. In other words, for every dollar you invest in your portfolio, you want to get two dollars back over time. And, if you want to be one of the top decile early stage investors, you want to shoot for a DPI of 3X or greater.

As we discuss in Chapter 5, a successful early stage investment portfolio has a mix of strikeouts, base hits and home runs. So how is it possible for an early stage investor to build a successful portfolio compiled from companies that produce such widely different financial returns? To answer that question, we pulled together a simple modeling tool that helps you visualize how the probable returns play out and interact to produce an overall portfolio return. As usual, we built it as a Google Sheet that allows you to make a copy and model a number of scenarios for your own portfolio.

How do you go about using this modeling tool? To start, we created a sample portfolio of 15 companies for you to work from. That's enough companies to begin with for a basic portfolio modeling exercise. For each company, there are two variables that you need to set.

- First, you will need to put in an **amount that you invest in each company**. In a portfolio of 15 companies, you might have the same amount invested in each company. Or, you might decide to distribute your investments in a less even fashion. In the default Google Sheet, we've set up a range of investment amounts. Some companies have as little as $15,000 invested and others have as much as $50,000.

- Second, you will need to chose or "model" the **type of exit for each company** in the portfolio. Here is where you determine the multiple of capital each company will return to your portfolio. Since we are dealing with early stage companies, you will have a real mix of returns. If you want a realistic model that will be predictive of probable real-life outcomes, we recommend that you set approximately half the portfolio to total losses (i.e. no capital returned). The rest of the portfolio can be a mix of moderate successes with maybe one or two bigger wins.

Investment Portfolio

			Type of Exit	Exit Multiple
Total Amount Invested	$500,000		Loss	0
Amount of Capital Returned	$1,335,000		Breakeven	1
Distributed to Paid-In (DPI) Capital Ratio	2.67		Base Hit	4
			Home Run	10
			Grand Slam	25

Individual Investments: Exit Types and Returns

Company Name	Total Investment	Percentage of Portfolio	Type of Exit	Total Amount Returned
Investment 1	$25,000	5%	Loss	$0
Investment 2	$50,000	10%	Base Hit	$200,000
Investment 3	$25,000	5%	Loss	$0
Investment 4	$15,000	3%	Base Hit	$60,000
Investment 5	$50,000	10%	Home Run	$500,000
Investment 6	$25,000	5%	Loss	$0
Investment 7	$15,000	3%	Loss	$0
Investment 8	$50,000	10%	Breakeven	$50,000
Investment 9	$25,000	5%	Base Hit	$100,000
Investment 10	$25,000	5%	Breakeven	$25,000
Investment 11	$25,000	5%	Loss	$0
Investment 12	$50,000	10%	Base Hit	$200,000
Investment 13	$50,000	10%	Base Hit	$200,000
Investment 14	$20,000	4%	Loss	$0
Investment 15	$50,000	10%	Loss	$0
Totals	**$500,000**	**100%**		**$1,335,000**

There is one other variable that you can control on this sheet. In the upper right quadrant of the sheet is a section for the Exit Multiple for each type of exit. We provide values for each exit type, but you might want to model using different exit multiples. So feel free to change these numbers to fit your needs.

Once you set the two variables for each company (and make any changes to the Exit Multiples), take a look in the upper left quadrant of the Google Sheet. There are three important metrics that are calculated for you in that section.

1. **Total Amount Invested**: This is the sum of all the investments you made in the portfolio and lists the total.

2. **Amount of Capital Returned**: This is the sum of all the returned capital based on the types of exits you set for each company.

3. **Distributed to Paid-In (DPI) Capital Ratio**: This represents the multiple of capital your portfolio returns. Remember, a solid DPI is 2 and a top quartile investor will have a DPI of 3 or greater.

As we discuss above, a DPI of 2X is a good target to aim for. And 3X is even better and puts you in league with the best VCs.

One final thought to keep in mind. This tool is helpful to determine your overall multiple of returned capital. However, it does not factor in the amount of time it took for this capital to be returned. As you are building your own early stage portfolio, make sure you watch out for how long it takes to get a return on your capital. If your returns take significantly more than 10 years to appear, your resulting IRR returns will be much less than optimal. You won't earn enough for the risk you are taking and you might be better off investing in the public stock markets!

III. Sample IRS Section 83(b) Election Form

Many years ago I joined the board of a company after my angel group became the lead investor in the company's seed financing round. As part of my compensation for being a board member, the company issued me restricted stock. Since I was new to the early stage investing world, I didn't understand what the tax implications were with restricted stock. It's unfortunate that I didn't get good tax planning advice at the time, because if I had, it would have saved me a significant amount on my tax bill when the company was acquired for a very significant price!

Fortunately, you don't have to make the same mistake I did. To help you avoid my fate, let's get started and provide you with some critical planning advice to help you put better plans in place. After you read this article, you should have a basic understanding of the following items:

- What is Restricted Stock?
- What is an IRS Section 83(b) Election?
- What do I need to do to file an 83(b) Election?
- What are the tax implications when you file an 83(b) Election?

Restricted Stock is given to employees, directors and advisors of early stage companies as a form of compensation. It's called restricted stock because your ownership rights are imperfect or restricted. There may be vesting conditions which need to lapse or there may be "restrictions" on when the shareholder is able to sell this stock. Most restricted stock grants require that the shareholder be active with the company for a certain number of years in order to fully own all of the restricted stock.

An **IRS Section 83(b) Election** is an approach to minimizing the amount of tax you will pay as you vest your stock. What you are basically doing is opting to pay taxes earlier than you have to (1) to lock in a low value at that time and (2) in exchange for a better rate later on. In effect, you declare ownership early, and pay ordinary income taxes on your ownership when the stock is less valuable and then later pay the lower capital gains tax rate on the increase in value.

How does this work? In the early days of a startup company, the fair market value of the stock is pretty low because the company isn't worth that much. Over time, the stock becomes more valuable as the company grows its revenues and builds value for its shareholders. Since restricted stock is treated as income by the IRS, it's best to recognize that income on your taxes when the company's stock is at a low value. Filing an 83(b) Election is allowing you to recognize, by approval of the IRS, the value of the restricted stock at the date of the election versus later as the stock vests.

Filing an 83(b) Election is not that complicated, but it does require a fair number of steps and it must be done in a very timely fashion. The first thing to be aware of is you must file your 83(b) Election **within 30 days of receiving the grant**. That's not much time to get your paperwork filed, but those are the rules! Now, here are all the steps you must take to make a proper election…

- Start by downloading a Sample IRS Section 83(b) Election Form. There are a few items you will need to know to fill out the form, including the fair market value price of the shares you are receiving and the total amount of income that will be added to your gross income.

- If you download this sample form, you will also notice a sample cover letter that you should fill out and include when you mail your 83(b) Election Form.

- Once you complete the 83(b) Election Form and the cover letter, you should mail them to the IRS Service Center where you typically file your federal income taxes. If you are a stickler about keeping tidy records, you can send your mail by certified mail and request a return receipt.

- **And, make sure you send these documents within 30 days of receiving the grant!**
- The final item on your task list is to mail a copy of the 83(b) Election Form to the company for their financial records.

It's also important that you understand the **tax implications when you file an 83(b) Election**. There are three types of tax rates you need to be aware of to understand how filing an 83(b) will affect the amount of tax you ultimately pay out.

- **Ordinary Income Tax Rate**: For high income individuals (which I assume includes most people who end up receiving restricted stock!), this tax rate is the highest rate you will pay. In 2016, the maximum rate was set at 39.6%.
- **Short Term Capital Gains Tax Rate**: If you sell your stock after holding it for less than one full year, you will pay taxes at the Short Term Rate. In 2016, your Short Term Rate was the same as your Ordinary Income Tax Rate.
- **Long Term Capital Gains Tax Rate**: If you sell your stock after holding it for more than one full year, you will pay taxes at the Long Term Rate. In 2016, the Long Term Rate was 20%.

One goal of filing an 83(b) Election is to limit the amount of taxes you pay while your stock is vesting. To illustrate how an 83(b) Election works for your taxes, let's walk through a very simple example.

- You receive a grant of 100,000 shares that are valued at $0.05 per share at the time of the grant. If you file an 83(b) Election within 30 days of this grant, you will need to include $5,000 of income on your taxes for that year. If you are in the highest tax bracket (39.6%), you will pay **$1,980 in Federal Taxes**.

Now, let's say you don't file an 83(b) Election. In this case, you will pay taxes over a four year period as follows.

- To keep this example as simple as possible, I will assume that your stock vests at a rate of 25% each year. So every year, you vest 25,000 shares. And, again to keep this simple, I will assume that the stock appreciates in value each year by $0.05 per share. That's a conservative assumption for a company that's doing reasonably well and showing solid growth.

- At the end of year one, you vest 25,000 shares and the price of those shares is $0.10 at the time of vesting. Your income for the year is $2,500 and you pay $990 in Federal Taxes (39.6% of $2,500).

- At the end of year two, three and four, you vest 25,000 shares each year. The price of the shares is $0.15 at year two, $0.20 at year three and $0.25 at year four. Your income for each of those years is $3,750, $5,000 and $6,250. And finally, your Federal tax payments are $1,485, $1,980 and $2,475.

- All told, you will pay **$6,930 in Federal Taxes** during the four year vesting period.

In this example, by filing an 83(b) Election, **you saved $4,950** on your Federal Tax bill. Not a bad savings for a few minutes of work!

There's one other potential large tax savings if you file an 83(b). That savings relates to a reduction of the Long Term Capital Gains tax you pay when holding stock for more than five years. This significant tax reduction is described in IRS Section 1202 of the US Federal Tax Code.

It's possible to pay no Long Term Capital Gains on your Federal tax return for stock held more than five years. By paying taxes on your restricted stock when you first receive the grant, you start the clock ticking on the five year holding period right away. If you wait to pay taxes on the stock at each year of vesting, you push out the five year holding period. So, for example, if the company is acquired 6 years after your initial restricted stock grant, you will pay no Federal capital gains on that stock if you filed an 83(b). If you didn't file an 83(b), you will pay Federal capital gains tax on the stock you vested in years 2, 3 and 4. And, that could be a BIG tax hit!!

Beware of the one downside to the 83(b) Election. If the company goes out of business a year or so after you file your 83(b), you will have paid taxes on value you will never receive, and you can't get those tax payments refunded.

Since taxes can be quite complicated, you should talk to your financial advisor / accountant to make sure you are doing the right thing given your personal financial situation.

Sample IRS Section 83(b) Election Form

ELECTION UNDER SECTION 83(b) OF THE
INTERNAL REVENUE CODE OF 1986, AS AMENDED

The undersigned taxpayer hereby elects, pursuant to Section 83(b) of the Internal Revenue Code of 1986, as amended, to include in his or her gross income for the current taxable year, the amount of any compensation taxable to him or her in connection with his or her receipt of the property described below:

The name, address, taxpayer identification number and taxable year of the undersigned are as follows:

NAME OF TAXPAYER: _____

TAXPAYER'S ADDRESS: _____

TAXPAYER ID#: _____

TAXABLE YEAR FOR WHICH ELECTION IS BEING MADE: Calendar year [Year]

1. The property with respect to which the election is made is described as follows: [Number of Shares] shares (the "Shares") of the Common Stock, $0.0001 par value per share, of [Name of Company], a [State of Incorporation] corporation (the "Company").

2. The date on which the property was transferred is: _____.

3. The nature of the restriction(s) to which the property is subject is: (a) taxpayer shall not sell, assign, transfer, pledge, hypothecate or otherwise dispose of, by operation of law or otherwise, any Shares, or any interest therein, that are not vested; and (b) in the event that the taxpayer ceases to be employed by or provide services to the Company before the Shares vest, the Company shall have the right and option to purchase from the taxpayer some or all of the Shares at a price equal to $0.0001 per share.

4. The fair market value at the time of transfer, determined without regard to any restriction other than a restriction which by its terms will never lapse, of such property is: [$X.XX] per share.

5. The amount, if any, paid by the taxpayer for such property: [$Y.YY] per share.

6. The amount to be included in the taxpayer's gross income is [$Z.ZZ].

The undersigned taxpayer will file this election with the Internal Revenue Service office with which taxpayer files his or her annual income tax return not later than 30 days after the date of transfer of the property. The undersigned will also submit a copy of this statement to the person for whom the services were performed in connection with the undersigned's receipt of the above-described property. The transferee of such property is the person performing the services in connection with the transfer of said property. Nothing contained herein shall be held to change any of the terms or conditions of the award agreement or the plan pursuant to which the Shares were granted.

The undersigned understand(s) that the foregoing election may not be revoked except with the consent of the Commissioner.

Dated: _____   _____

[Name], Taxpayer

The undersigned spouse of taxpayer joins in this election.

Dated: _____   _____

_____, Spouse of Taxpayer

Sample Cover Letter for IRS Section 83(b) Election

Department of the Treasury
IRS Service Center
[Address of IRS Office where you mail your taxes]

To Whom It May Concern:

Enclosed with this letter is an executed original of the IRS Section 83(b) Election under the Internal Revenue Code of 1986, as amended. This Election Form is filed for:

Name: _____

SSN: _____

Sincerely,

[Name]

This book is brought to you by the founders of **Seraf.** Seraf is a web-based portfolio management tool for investors in early stage companies. Seraf's intuitive dashboard gives angel investors the power to organize all of their angel activities in one online workspace. With Seraf, investors can see the combined value of their holdings, monitor company progress, analyze key performance metrics, track tax issues, store investment documents in a cloud-based digital locker, and more. Seraf's easy interface enables investors to track their early stage portfolios as efficiently as they track their public investments. To learn more, visit **Seraf-Investor.com**.

Hambleton Lord is Co-Founder of Seraf and the Co-Managing Director of Launchpad Venture Group, an angel investment group focused on seed and early-stage investments in technology-oriented companies. Ham has built a personal portfolio of more than 60 early stage investments and is a board member, advisor and mentor to numerous start-ups.

Seraf Co-Founder **Christopher Mirabile** is the Chair Emeritus of the Angel Capital Association and also Co-Managing Director of Launchpad Venture Group. He has personally invested in over 75 start-up companies and is a limited partner in four specialized angel funds. Christopher is a frequent panelist and speaker on entrepreneurship and angel-related topics and serves as an adjunct lecturer in Entrepreneurship in the MBA program at Babson. Due to their combination of roles as investors, advisors and angel group leaders, Ham and Christopher were named among Xconomy's "Top Angel Investors in New England."

Made in the USA
Columbia, SC
02 August 2019